FULL OF OURSELVES

A Wellness Program to Advance Girl Power, Health, and Leadership

FULL OF OURSELVES

A Wellness Program to Advance Girl Power, Health, and Leadership

Catherine Steiner-Adair and Lisa Sjostrom

Teachers College, Columbia University
New York and London

The "Catch" icebreaker is used with permission of the Cambridge Prevention Coalition. The activity originally appeared in CPC's 7th Grade Alcohol, Tobacco and Other Drug Prevention Unit.

"Body Statues" is based on the "Act Like a Lady/Act Like a Man" activity in *Working It Out*, a curriculum published in conjunction with Take Our Daughters to Work Day, by Lisa Sjostrom (New York: Ms. Foundation for Women, 1993).

"Tree of Strength" is based on the "Following Footsteps" activity in *Working It Out*, a curriculum published in conjunction with Take Our Daughters to Work Day, by Lisa Sjostrom (New York: Ms. Foundation for Women, 1993).

Published by Teachers College Press, 1234 Amsterdam Avenue, New York, NY 10027

ISBN-13: 978-0-8077-4631-8 (paper)   ISBN-10: 0-8077-4631-2 (paper)

Printed on acid-free paper
Manufactured in the United States of America

13   8   7   6   5   4

Contents

Acknowledgments

We extend heartfelt thanks to the thousands of people who contributed to the creation of Full of Ourselves (FOO).

First, we want to express our personal and professional thanks to Carol Gilligan and Alexendra Merril, two early mentors who taught us worlds about girls' psychology and group process.

In 1997, David Herzog created the Harvard Eating Disorders Center (HEDC), where this project began. There we joined forces with many talented colleagues, including Anne Becker, Deborah Franko, Kim McCabe, visiting scholar Susan Paxton, Trisha Guest, and dedicated interns. We thank all of them for their theoretical wisdom and collegial support.

With great appreciation, we thank the HEDC Board of Directors, who gave generously of their time and were, each in his or her own way, important supporters of the development of this curriculum—among them Joel Alvord, Susan Blumenthal, Austin Cable, Eunice Cohen, Joseph Coyle, Dick Floor, Eleanor Friedman, Gladys Jacober, Jill Karp, Seth Klarman, Michael Moskow, Carol Pierce, and Barbara Salter.

In 2003, we relocated and joined forces with the Department of Psychology at McLean Hospital, a Harvard Medical School affiliate. We thank our many supportive colleagues at our new home, including Bruce Cohen, Phil Levendusky, Peter Paskovich, Evelyn Morse, Cathie Cook, and Gil Noam and his team at the RALLY project, who share our commitment to school-based primary prevention efforts. We extend special thanks to Beth and Seth Klarman for their support of our work, for their inspirational leadership in founding the Klarman Eating Disorder Center at McLean, and for their help in finding us this new home for our project.

Although the field of eating disorders prevention is quite new, we've benefited greatly from the work of predecessors in the field, especially that of Michael Levine and Linda Smolak, Niva Piran, Ruth Streigel-Moore, Diana Flescher, Diane Neumark-Sztainer, and Kathy Kater.

We convened a FOO advisory board comprised of exceptional people, all experts in their various fields. We'd like to thank this dynamic group for their helpful input throughout the development of the project, including Niva Piran, Michael Levine, Bryn Austin, Amy Purcell-Vorenberg, Kevin Thompson, and, in particular, Susan Willard, who has been our biggest advocate and a continual source of wisdom.

We extend special thanks to our funders. In 1997, we received a generous gift from the Paul and Phyllis Fireman Charitable Foundation as part of their larger Girls Action Initiative. The Firemans got us up and running and have been our strongest backers ever since. We also extend gratitude to four other foundations that have given generous support: the Claneil Foundation, the Klarman Family Foundation, the Rutland Corner Foundation, and the Weyerhaueser Family Foundation.

Program evaluation is a costly and arduous undertaking. While there are hundreds of eating disorders education and prevention programs available, only a handful have been extensively evaluated. Without a thorough evaluation, it's hard to know if a curriculum actually achieves what it sets out to do; and some, unintentionally, do more harm than good.

We extensively evaluated the FOO program over a 5-year period and brought superb people on board to help us do so. First and foremost, we acknowledge program evaluators Seeta Pai and Rochelle Tucker, who pored over thousands of questionnaires and made sense of data. We thank them for their tireless dedication.

We field-tested the program in a dozen Boston-area schools and organizations before gearing up for a major pilot study involving 26 schools across New England and an entire school district in Tulsa, Oklahoma. These two rounds of studies involved more than 1,000 girls and 150 adult leaders—teachers, guidance counselors, school nurses, librarians, and moms—who led program sessions, administered three rounds of questionnaires, and offered us invaluable feedback. We thank them for their time, commitment, creativity, and hard work.

We offer special recognition to three site leaders in particular. Nancy Beardall has been with us from the start. A gifted teacher, dance therapist, and Wellness and Prevention counselor in the Newton public school system, Nancy led many FOO groups, involved student interns, and helped us to revamp various curriculum activities. Joanne Linden, a psychologist currently at Pastoral Counseling Services in Manchester, single-handedly recruited all of our New Hampshire sites, 11 schools in all, and oversaw a dedicated cadre of site leaders. Kelly Dudney, our wonderful colleague at the Junior League of Tulsa, coordinated a mammoth effort involving 7 public and private schools in the Tulsa metropolitan area. We thank these women for giving so much of their time and themselves to this work.

We also extend special thanks to Karin Lindfors and Silvy Brooks of the Winsor School in Boston for providing the prototype for the sample letters to parents; to nutritionist Lisa Pearl for her expert input on Unit 6, especially the "Snack Attack!" handout; and to yoga instructor Isa Mattei of Sun-Moon Yoga for consultation on the yoga activities.

We offer a rousing round of applause to our 40 pilot sites, including school superintendents and principals who gave FOO their stamp of approval and parents who signed permission slips and gave us feedback on our parent guide.

Bigelow Middle School, Newton, MA
Blanchard Middle School, Westford, MA
Cascia Hall, Tulsa, OK
Dana Hall School, Wellesley, MA
Deerfield Middle School, Deerfield, NH
Derryfield School, Manchester, NH
Edward Devotion School, Brookline, MA
F. A. Day Middle School, Newton, MA
Girls Inc. of Lynn, Lynn, MA
Greenwich Academy, Greenwich, CT
Holland Hall, Tulsa, OK
Hopkinton Middle/High, Hopkinton, NH
Jenks East Middle School, Tulsa, OK
Jenks 7th and 8th Grade Center, Tulsa, OK
Kearsage Middle School, New London, NH
Lawrence School, Brookline, MA
Londonderry Middle School, Londonderry, NH
Memorial Middle School, Laconia, NH
Merrimack Valley Middle School, Penacook, NH
Metro Christian Academy, Tulsa, OK
Milton Academy, Milton, MA
Monte Cassino, Tulsa, OK
Newton Country Day School of the Sacred
    Heart, Newton, MA
Newton Free Library, Newton, MA
O'Maley Middle School, Gloucester, MA
Peirce School, Brookline, MA
Pittsfield Middle School, Pittsfield, NH
Plymouth Middle School, Plymouth, NH
Portsmouth Middle School, Portsmouth, NH
R. J. Grey Junior High, Acton, MA
Rundlett Middle School, Concord, NH
School of St. Mary, Tulsa, OK
Shady Hill School, Cambridge, MA
Telstar Middle School, Bethel, ME
Union Middle School, Tulsa, OK
Waltham Family YMCA of Greater Boston,
    Waltham, MA
West Middle School, Andover, MA
West Newton Unitarian Universalist Society,
    Newton, MA
Windham Middle School, Windham, ME
Winsor School, Boston, MA

Finally, we dedicate the FOO program to the hundreds of girls who participated in the pilot program and took the time to tell us what worked, what didn't, and why. Their stories moved us and moved this program into the world to the benefit of girls everywhere.

Introduction

Over the last few years, it has become increasingly clear that America's children struggle far too often and far too early with disordered eating and eating disorders. Anorexia, bulimia, and obesity are all on the increase. Eating disorders rank as one of the most common chronic psychiatric illnesses among young women, and their prevalence among teenage and preteen girls is growing. On the other end of the spectrum, childhood obesity has reached troubling proportions.

This serious scenario makes evident the need for large-scale health education and eating disorders prevention efforts. It is imperative that we invest in effective ways to equip children—and the adults who can potentially make a significant difference in their lives—with tools to resist cultural directives toward body preoccupation, overeating, and disordered eating behaviors.

Welcome to Full of Ourselves, our clear-cut response to this need! FOO is an upbeat educational program that aims to sustain girls in their mental, physical, and social health and to decrease their vulnerability to the development of body preoccupation and eating disorders. As a primary prevention program, FOO targets a general (healthy) population of girls; no one need be at risk for an eating disorder to participate. FOO has been successfully implemented by schools, after-school programs, town libraries, summer camps, churches, and synagogues. All that's needed is a supportive community and one or two committed women to facilitate weekly program sessions. (While it's not inconceivable that a man could be a co-leader, we've found that teenage girls are best able to be honest and take risks in the presence of women rather than men.)

The program has been piloted with more than 800 girls in five states and been proven feasible and effective. This is the first prevention program of its kind to effect sustained positive changes in girls' body image, body satisfaction, and body-esteem, important risk factors in the development of eating disorders. The program also results in sustained positive changes in girls' knowledge about health, nutrition, weightism, and puberty. It is most effective when administered grade-wide rather than to a select subset of girls within a given grade. When all girls are on the same page, they can reinforce newly gained ideas and skills outside of program sessions; the resulting "environmental" effect may make it easier for girls to sustain long-lasting positive behavioral change.

While FOO was not initially designed as an obesity prevention program, it implements many of the recent recommendations from the Institute of Medicine on how to stem the growing obesity problem. For starters, girls learn how to eat healthfully and exercise more. They learn how to identify media messages and advertisements that are harmful to their physical or psychological well-being. They discuss the pitfalls of eating in an attempt to fill purely emotional hungers, and then learn healthier ways to deal with emotions and stress. The program also encourages overweight girls not to turn to fad diets, but rather to get healthy guidance and support.

Our program title, Full of Ourselves, invariably generates lots of questions. Just what do you mean by "full of ourselves," people ask, when the term is commonly used pejoratively? We knew the research. When you ask boys to identify their strengths and things about themselves that make them proud, without pause they launch into a list of things they can do in the world: "I'm great at math . . . I'm a team captain . . . I throw a killer fastball . . . I design computer programs. . . ." Ask girls the same question and often you are met with a pause. Or giggles. Or silence. Some girls, like their male counterparts, answer without hesitation. But many don't. Many flat-out refuse to answer or avoid answering directly:

"Ask Mia, she's my best friend." Girls frequently offer up a list of physical attributes: "I have great hair . . . I like my eyes . . . I have long legs. . . ." Others talk easily about relational skills—"I'm a good friend . . . I'm a good listener"—but are less comfortable talking about intellectual prowess and skill-based activities at which they excel.

Why is it, we asked ourselves, that at the turn into the 21st century so many girls struggle to claim their strengths? Why do so many girls, unlike many boys, hesitate to take up their rightful space in the world?

Girls are growing up in a popular culture and an economy that continue to send them the message that what they look like is more important than who they are. In some communities, being the "prettiest" girl means being the thinnest; in others, being the curviest; and in others, being the most "buff." While the ideal image may vary, what remains sadly consistent is just how many girls refer to their bodies as *the* ultimate measure of their worth: Many girls literally weigh their self-esteem. This focus on bodies as a primary source of identity predisposes girls to disordered thinking and to disordered eating, which can escalate into a full-blown eating disorder and serious health problems. Disordered eating also disrupts learning; when a girl diets, skips meals, or subsists mainly on junk food, she's not getting the nourishment she needs to think and to perform at her best.

This curriculum aims to give girls an entirely different lens through which to see, know, and value themselves. The focus remains throughout, as indicated in the subtitle, on power, health, and leadership.

Power

Girls learn how to tune into their bodies as sources of strength and practice the radical act of body acceptance. They learn how to powerfully state their own opinions. They learn about the power that comes from creating and sustaining healthy connections with others. They learn the basics of assertiveness training, conflict resolution, and strategies to stand up in the face of mean teasing or bullying. They also learn to practice positive self-talk, which has been shown to boost self-esteem; the ways we talk to ourselves can profoundly influence how we feel.

Health

Girls gain tools to build and sustain the well-being of body, mind, and spirit. Girls learn how to eat more nutritiously. They come to understand the difference between "dieting" and having a healthy diet, as well as how to replace the rigid notion of "good" versus "bad" foods with the idea of more or less "powerful" foods. Equally important, girls learn how *not* to use food as a coping mechanism; they learn a variety of stress-reduction techniques—meditation, journaling, yoga—to help them stay balanced in any situation. Girls also examine the dynamics of relationships and learn how "relational health" affects their overall well-being.

Leadership

Throughout the program, girls have the chance to experience themselves as leaders and agents of change. Every unit concludes with a "Call to Action," asking girls to "walk the talk" and put ideas into action out in the world of family and peers. For example, girls learn effective ways to intervene when they hear anyone being excluded or put down for the way they look; they write letters (of protest or praise) to advertisers and editors of fashion magazines; they assess the cafeteria menu and submit findings and recommendations to school administrators. In the second program phase, girls become mentors and lead activities with younger girls. Research on primary prevention makes clear that when students have the opportunity to teach what they've learned, they are more likely actually to practice what they preach.

It is our hope that, by the end of this two-phase program, girls will not only be less vulnerable to the development of an eating disorder but also be "full of themselves" in the *very best* sense of the phrase. In the first unit, girls discuss and declare a "Full of Ourselves" proclamation; here is what a girl or woman who is full of herself, in the best sense of the phrase, might say:

- I know who I am.
- I know that I matter.
- I know what matters to me.
- I pay attention to what I feel and what I need.
- I make choices and decisions that are good for me.
- I take good care of my body.
- I stand up for what I believe in.
- I let people know what I think, even when I'm angry or confused or in disagreement with everyone else.
- I am a valuable friend.
- I know I can make a positive difference in the world in my own unique way.

We have spent 5 years developing, evaluating, and fine-tuning this curriculum. It is written with great attention to detail to make the units accessible and easy for you to teach. We invite you to read on, to have fun, and, along with your group of girls, to throw your weight around in healthy ways!

❀ Program Objectives ❀

At the end of the program, girls ideally will demonstrate the following:

1. Increased self-acceptance and body acceptance
2. Higher levels of self-esteem and confidence
3. A greater sense of agency and efficacy
4. Advanced leadership skills
5. A recognition of "weightism" as a form of prejudice and the courage to speak up in face of weightist teasing and bullying
6. A wider range of coping skills to use in response to stressful or emotional situations
7. The ability to discern the difference between physiological and emotional hungers
8. Healthier eating and exercise habits
9. A proficiency with basic media literacy skills
10. A decreased vulnerability to developing an eating disorder

Preparing to Lead the Program: Commonly Asked Questions

What types of organizations can use Full of Ourselves?

The program has been successfully implemented by all kinds of organizations, including schools, after-school programs, town libraries, summer camps, churches, and synagogues. All that's needed is a supportive community and one or two committed adult women to facilitate group sessions over 2–4 months.

How is the program organized?

The program has two distinct phases geared toward different age groups of girls. During phase 1, a group of 6th, 7th, or 8th graders (11- to 14-year-olds) completes the eight Full of Ourselves units under the guidance of one or two women leaders. The group meets once or twice per week for 45–60 minutes. It's best not to meet daily so that girls have time to complete "Call to Action" assignments outside of class.

During phase 2, these same girls become peer leaders and lead one to five Throw Your Weight Around sessions with 4th or 5th graders (8- to 10-year-olds).

This publication includes everything you need to complete both the two program phases: the eight Full of Ourselves units, along with two Throw Your Weight Around guides—one for adults, one for girls.

Who are the girl participants? Do they need to have an eating disorder to attend?

This prevention program is aimed at a general (i.e., healthy) population of girls; no one need be "at risk" for an eating disorder to participate. The program works well with 6th, 7th, and 8th graders alike. Every group member needs to make a commitment to attend all of the sessions; this is *not* a drop-in program. At the start, girls should double-check that they won't run into a scheduling conflict with sports or other activities. Girls may or may not know each other beforehand.

❀ Pointers from Past Leaders ❀

1. We had eight girls, with plenty of time to talk. Fifteen would be too many.
2. Be prepared to learn.
3. Expect many unexpected conversations.
4. Prepare at least 1 day in advance. The group is more enjoyable if you are organized.
5. Model willingness to tackle meaty topics.
6. Be sensitive to your own issues about your body and keep these to yourself.
7. Connection with the girls is most important. The curriculum comes second.
8. Quality, not quantity! Make a commitment to end activities with discussion before moving on.
9. Let the girls do as much leading as possible. Don't lecture the information. Pull it out of the girls.
10. Biggest challenge: getting the girls not to all talk at once.

How large is a Full of Ourselves group?

Ideal group size is 8 to 12 girls.

What's the best way to attract girls to the program?

Don't bill it as an eating disorders prevention program. Instead, place emphasis on girl power, health, peer relationships, and leadership. (This program does build self-esteem, but this word is often overused!) Middle-schoolers tend to get excited about designing and leading sessions with younger girls.

Does this program work for girls from all racial and ethnic backgrounds?

This program helps girls from all backgrounds. It increases their body- and self-esteem, body acceptance, knowledge, and so on. You know your population of girls better than anyone, so feel free to tailor the language and ideas to best suit your girls.

Some of the African-American girls I work with don't care about being skinny. Is this curriculum relevant for these girls?

One of the wonderful advantages of having a racially diverse group of girls is that you'll likely hear from many of them that larger or curvier women are considered beautiful in their communities. This curriculum doesn't define one standard of beauty; rather, we question *all* rigid standards of beauty. Our goal is to help girls move beyond the notion that they need to achieve a certain look—be that unnaturally skinny or unnaturally curvy—in order to be considered attractive and lovable. Beautiful bodies come in all shapes and sizes! The challenge is to maintain the healthiest bodies we can, through healthy exercise and eating, given our genetic predispositions.

I worry that certain factors in my school may counteract the good work I plan to do with girls: for example, vending machines stocked with soda and junk food, boys' macho attitudes toward girls, teachers who are unaware of these issues, and so on.

Before you begin your group, it definitely pays to try to create as supportive a school setting as possible, one that concurrently addresses risk factors for disordered eating and body preoccupation and promotes protective factors. Aim to get as many staff members on board as possible, administrators as well as teachers. For starters, request time at a faculty meeting to present the major themes of the program and carefully review the 10 Tips for Schools section of this book (Addendum E).

Who should lead the program sessions?

One or, preferably, two women are needed to facilitate group sessions. You can be teachers, counselors, nurses, after-school personnel, therapists: anyone who shares a commitment to girls' healthy development and to the ideas presented in this curriculum. You also must be available and willing to dedicate 2 to 4 months to this educational endeavor. Because the program is largely discussion-based, it is

important that group leaders have experience with guiding discussions. *Guide* is the operative word. Think of yourselves as guides rather than teachers.

What happens with younger girls during phase 2 of the program?

This is where some of the most profound learning takes place. The 6th, 7th, or 8th graders, now peer leaders, design and lead anywhere from one to five sessions for 4th- or 5th-grade girls. They draw on suggested activities in a second curriculum guide titled *Throw Your Weight Around: A Guide for Girl Leaders*. There is an accompanying Throw Your Weight Around guide for adult leaders as well. In the best of all possible worlds, when the younger girls reach middle school they will have the opportunity to participate in Full of Ourselves sessions and become peer leaders themselves.

How do I plan for program phase 2, Throw Your Weight Around?

Start planning for the Throw Your Weight Around sessions at the very start. Recruit the group of younger girls: a 3rd-, 4th-, or 5th-grade class from a local elementary school, members of a Brownie troop, and so on. Set dates. Arrange for transportation if needed.

At the start of the Full of Ourselves units, tell the older girls about the second phase of the program. Girls tend to take the sessions more seriously when you remind them that soon they'll be the teachers and leaders. You can turn difficult moments to advantage by asking questions such as this: How will you work with 4th graders if they get bored? Do you think a 4th grader will understand this? How could you say this in words a younger girl would understand? For details, refer to *Throw Your Weight Around: A Guide for Adult Leaders.*

How long does the program take to complete in its entirety?

The program lasts anywhere from 2 to 4 months, depending on three factors: (1) length of group meetings, (2) frequency of group meetings, and (3) the number of sessions with younger girls in program phase 2. Each of the eight Full of Ourselves units takes 45 to 60 minutes to complete.

Let's say you can devote a full hour to each weekly session. In this case, phase 1 will take at least 8 weeks. (Girls like to talk, so it's best to plan for one or two spillover sessions.) If you meet twice a week for 1 hour, phase 1 will take at least 4 weeks. If you have less than an hour and aim to complete all of the activities, anticipate adding several extra meetings. Phase 2 consists of anywhere from one to five Throw Your Weight Around sessions with younger girls. Count on one planning session prior to each TYWA session.

Do I need to read the scripts word for word?

Italicized scripts are designed to help you introduce new topics, convey key ideas, segue between activities, and wrap up meetings. Feel free to rephrase these in your own words.

Is it necessary to teach the program units in order?

Yes, the eight Full of Ourselves units are mapped out purposefully and should be taught in sequence over consecutive weeks. Each unit contains "core" and "supplemental" activities. Core activities are required and provide the underpinnings for effective prevention. Supplemental activities provide girls with a chance to deepen their understanding of given topics. As your time allows, we encourage you to try one or more supplemental activities in each unit.

What if we don't complete an entire unit in a single meeting?

Each program unit is designed to be taught within a 60-minute session—if you move at a steady pace with no unexpected interruptions. In a room full of teenage girls, however, the one thing you can expect is the unexpected! On a given day, one or two activities may occupy an entire session; on another day, you may complete all core activities. As your calendar allows, take as much time as needed to complete each unit. Rushing through an activity or preempting discussion defeats an important program goal—allowing girls the needed space to be full of themselves. The issues at hand are often complex, and it's important to try to hold on to this complexity. So if it's "time to move on" and girls are engaged in conversation, use your discretion. Sometimes you may want to allow for a digression; girls report that digressions often lead to the most important conversations.

Can I lead the program if I'm struggling with my own weight-related issues?

Absolutely. We expect every woman involved in the program, regardless of her age or personal weight-related issues, to get stirred up by these lessons in any number of ways. Be prepared for this. Review the "10 Tips for Parents" (Addendum C) and take time to answer the questions about your own body image and attitudes. Read through the curriculum *before* you begin working with girls so that, during group meetings, you can be available explicitly for them. Try the lessons on for size, paying close attention to any resistance you have to messages in the curriculum. If you are working with a co-leader, you might want to discuss the ways the lessons affect you personally. During a meeting, it is best not to discuss your own history with food, dieting, or other body-related topics. You are a facilitator, not a group participant. However, if girls ask you a personal question and you choose to respond, try to meet girls "where they're at" and to match your response to their level of depth and disclosure. Keep in mind that anything you say in the group may travel, even when confidentiality has been promised! It is our hope that this program will help you, as well as girls, resist the cultural prescriptions toward body criticism and embolden you to take respectful care of yourself.

How do I fit this program into a busy schoolday?

Schools carve out time in different ways. Girls can be excused from other classes to attend group sessions. The curriculum can be adopted as part of Health class, with boys working in a single-sex group on a separate topic. Full of Ourselves can be offered as an extracurricular activity before school, after school, or during lunch period (girls bring lunch to group). Guidance counselors can run a Full of Ourselves group. Whatever the case in your school, ask your principal to send a general notice to all staff describing the program and any disruption it may or may not cause. This step is crucial when girls will attend group sessions in lieu of other classes or activities. Under no circumstance should girls have to contend with flak from other teachers.

I plan to work with a co-leader. Is there anything special we should know?

Take some time to get to know one another—your strengths and weaknesses, your similarities and differences, your skills and working styles—and discuss how you each can best contribute to group meetings. Before each meeting, take time to discuss the flow of activities and to divvy up your roles and responsibilities. Afterwards, debrief: Share your perceptions, discuss problematic moments, and brainstorm what you might have done differently. Girls may inadvertently test co-leaders in an attempt to determine who is "really" in charge. For example, they may play favorites or play the two of you off each other. Resist these efforts. You are a team, and it is critical for girls to see women working supportively—even when you have different opinions! One last thing: Don't hesitate to ask each other for help, both privately and in front of the girls.

Is it okay to change the program name?

Yes, but it's important to be aware of the thinking behind the name "Full of Ourselves." Here's a simple, yet illustrative, story. While doing research in elementary, middle, and high schools, we often thank the girls by getting them pizza for lunch. When asked what they want on their pizzas, 10-year-olds typically say, without hesitation, "extra cheese with pepperoni," 13-year-olds say, "I don't know," and 15-year-olds say "whatever." Studies indicate that many girls become reluctant to state their preferences and opinions as they enter adolescence—from matters as simple as what they'd like to eat to matters as serious as whether they welcome boys' sexual advances. The program name is intended to serve as a counterweight to this unhealthy tendency. That said, if your girls' dislike of the program name threatens their enjoyment of the sessions, invite the girls to rename the group to "make it your own." Some examples of alternative names girls have chosen in the past: Girl Power, Planet Girl, That's PHAT (Putting Health Above Thinness).

Should Full of Ourselves be a graded academic course?

We never intended for this program to be graded. However, we recognize that schools may require some form of evaluation. Before getting started, decide how and to what degree you will hold girls accountable for their participation in the group. In some instances, girls may take the program more seriously if it is a graded course with required homework. In other instances, girls may jump at the chance to be part of a meaningful all-girl group that feels *nothing* like an academic class.

What should I do if a girl discloses that she has an eating disorder?

Unless you're a qualified professional, talk to your school nurse or counselor about how to proceed. As a precautionary measure, talk with them before the start of the program about appropriate protocol and what resources are available in your community.

How does physical activity figure into the program?

The program features several "body work" activities to get girls up and moving—or quietly tuning inward. As your time and motivation allow, we encourage you to incorporate more physical activities into the program. Strive to get across this message: Whatever your body shape and size, it can be fun to move and exercise.

Do I have to have prior experience to lead the yoga activities?

Prior experience with yoga is a plus, but not a prerequisite, for teaching girls some basic postures. Addendum A, "Yoga Primer," provides detailed instructions about how to get into and out of simple standing, warrior, and relaxation poses. Note that the "Yoga Primers" are not required; they supplement Units 2, 4, and 7. That said, we hope that you and the girls will have fun trying some yoga to help you find balance, stand your ground, and summon strength—literally and metaphorically.

What do I do when girls all start talking at once?

Freewriting is a simple technique you can use if all the girls are talking or no one's saying a word. Weave spontaneous writing into sessions at any point, particularly when group dynamics become heated or if certain girls monopolize conversation. Ask girls to put their pens to paper to focus their thoughts, respond to a comment, or express feelings that might get lost in the louder discussion. You can allow the writing to remain private or ask for volunteers to read freewrites aloud.

What about the boys?

Boys may be curious about what the girls are doing in this special group. We suggest that you schedule an info session at the end of Full of Ourselves where the girls can share key learnings with the boys.

What are some ways to get parents involved?

Parental support and involvement strengthen overall program effectiveness. Here are four ways to keep parents in the loop:

1. Organize a parent orientation night. Explain program goals, try out a few activities, and answer outstanding questions.
2. Hand out copies of "10 Tips for Parents" (Addendum C) at the orientation or send this home after your first session.
3. Send home periodic letters or e-mails to update parents on group progress. (See Addendum D.)
4. Help girls organize a celebratory FOO session for their moms, dads, and/or other important adults in their lives. Set a date near the end of program phase 1 and design invitations for girls to hand-deliver to invitees. Then help girls choose favorite activities to lead at the celebratory session.

Part One

Full of Ourselves

Unit One:
Full of Ourselves

ACTIVITIES

Core Activities
> Program Introduction
> Personal Introductions
> Ground Rules
> Full of Ourselves: A Brainstorm
> Confidence and Power: A Freewrite
> Body Scan: A Guided Meditation
> Call to Action Assignment
> Closing Circle

Supplemental Activities
> Jumpstart: Catch!
> Body Statues
> Picture This: A Symbolic Drawing
> Bioenergetic Punches

OBJECTIVES

- Introduce girls to the program, to one another, and to adult leaders.
- Establish ground rules to help ensure order, unity, and respectful behavior.
- Explore multiple meanings of the program title.
- Introduce body-centered activities.
- Convey the importance of putting ideas into action.

MATERIALS AND PREPARATION

- ☐ Supply nametags if the girls aren't acquainted.
- ☐ Supply pocket folders, one per girl.
- ☐ Supply "blue books" or spiral-bound notebooks for use as journals.
- ☐ Supply healthy snacks—perhaps bagels and juice if you meet in the morning; cheese, apples, baby carrots, or nuts if you meet in the afternoon.
- ☐ *Optional:* Bring in fresh flowers to celebrate the group's inauguration.
- ☐ Familiarize yourself with activities beforehand, highlighting key points and phrasing.
- ☐ *Note:* Handouts for all eight units can be found in Part Two.
- ☐ Photocopy the "Full of Ourselves Proclamation" (H-1A) and cut out one square per girl.
- ☐ Photocopy one "Call to Action" handout (H-1B) per girl.
- ☐ If you're meeting in a classroom, think of ways to create a nonacademic atmosphere for the group sessions; for example, gather around a pretty tablecloth laid down on the floor.
- ☐ Set up the room before the girls arrive. For example, lay a tablecloth on the floor, place flowers and snacks in the center, and set journals and pocket folders in front of each place.
- ☐ Spell out basic ground rules on newsprint. Leave space at the bottom for rules to be added by the girls and space around the edges for the girls to trace the outlines of their hands. Example:

Ground Rules

- Everyone's welcome.
- Everyone's needed: Be on time and attend all group sessions.
- What we say here is confidential.
- Show respect.
- Everyone gets to talk and express herself.
- No names! Refer to people generally.
- Disagreement's okay, but not judgment.
- Use "I" statements to give feedback ("I think," "I feel").

CORE ACTIVITIES

Program Introduction
(Time Estimate: 5 minutes)

⟳ Sit in a circle and welcome girls to the group. Hand out nametags if girls don't know one another. There are five points to touch upon at the start:

1. This is a group about power, health, and leadership. In this group, we're going to explore what it takes to be confident, healthy, and a leader in our individual lives, with our friends and family, and in the wider world.

2. We're going to do lots of fun activities together—role plays, collages, games, skits, journal writing—and take time to talk about all sorts of topics related to power, health, and leadership.

3. This group is about action. The way to make a difference in the world is to put what we're learning into practice. So every group will end with a "call to action."

4. We're in this together. We have a lot to learn from each other—and from all the things that make us different. Some of you may not know each other very well, and you might not all be best friends outside the group. But here, every one of you matters and all of your experiences count.

5. You're training to be leaders. At the end of these sessions, you'll have the chance to design and lead sessions with younger girls. So you're here for yourself and for the next generation of girls who look to you to lead the way.

⟳ Answer any questions. It's crucial that girls feel comfortable with the premise of the program.

☞ *Teaching Note:* If girls ask whether this is a program about eating disorders, the answer is "No, not exactly." The program doesn't directly discuss or define eating disorders, although you and the girls may decide to. The program focuses on how to be healthy and self-confident. Our belief is this: A girl who has learned how to respond to stress and diffi-

❊ Nutritional Awareness ❊

Make one or two seemingly off-the-cuff comments about the nutritional value of each snack. For example, "These baby carrots are great for your skin, loaded with vitamin A. So are the almonds, packed with vitamin E." This is a light-handed way to raise girls' nutritional awareness.

culties in direct, healthy ways isn't likely to use food as a coping mechanism. And she's not likely to want to change her body to feel better about herself because she knows that dieting and binge-eating aren't lasting solutions for building self-esteem, making friends, and so on. (For background information on eating disorders, see Addendum B.)

🕐 *Time Check:* If girls are not already acquainted and you have an extra 5–10 minutes, include the supplemental "Catch!" activity, a fun, physical way to break the ice.

Personal Introductions
(Time Estimate: 10 minutes)

☞ *Teaching Note:* Don't skip this activity, even if girls are already acquainted. Explain that they will come to know one another, as well as old concepts, in new ways over the course of the program. Thus, it's crucial that everyone keep an open and curious mind, especially about old friends.

⟳ Ask girls to pair up with someone they don't know very well. Form a trio if there is an odd number of girls. Explain the assignment:

1. Each person take a turn to introduce yourself to your partner. First, tell her your preferred name and your astrological sign.

2. Then tell her two things about yourself—things that are important to you in some way—that your partner doesn't already know and couldn't possibly know by just looking at you. For example, maybe you'll tell her about someone or something you care about, or a hidden talent, or something

that makes you really mad, or what you dream of accomplishing.

3. Begin with the following sentence: "If you knew me better, you'd know that . . ."

⊃ If you're working with a co-leader, model the introductions. For example, "My favorite cat, Pebbles, died last year, and I'm still sad" or "I've always wanted to learn how to sky-dive, and I've finally found the courage!"

⊃ Allow girls 3–4 minutes to complete their introductions.

⊃ Afterwards, go around and ask each pair to introduce themselves to the larger group. Each girl should introduce her partner (not herself) *if* her partner feels comfortable being introduced.

Sample wrap-up:

❝ Each of us is so interesting. We carry worlds inside of us that no one else could possibly guess without taking the time to really know us—from the inside out. In other words, our outward appearance isn't everything. I'm not saying that looks don't matter. But ask yourself this question: *What matters most?*❞

Ground Rules

(Time Estimate: 5 minutes)

⊃ Refer girls to your prepared sheet of ground rules:

❝ As you can already tell, sometimes we'll be talking about personal things here. So this needs to be a safe space for every one of us to talk and be ourselves. Here are some guidelines that other girls have suggested who've already been through this program. See what you think.❞

⊃ Each girl reads one ground rule aloud. Make sure that there is general understanding and consensus on each point. Ask generally: Any questions? Is this a good idea? Need modification? All in agreement? As useful, draw from the clarifying questions below.

Clarifying questions:

1. *Everyone's welcome:* Are some of you closer friends than others? What can we do to make sure everyone feels welcome and part of the group?

2. *Confidentiality:* Is it okay to talk about what happens in the group with people outside of the group? What about your parents? Is it okay to tell them particulars?

3. *Respect:* What does this word mean, exactly? (Respect of each other's bodies, clothes, feelings, opinions, cultural backgrounds, etc.) What about put-downs? Flip remarks? Judgment and criticism? What about joking? Is there such a thing as a "joke" about someone's body or the way she looks?

4. *Self-expression:* What if you notice that someone hasn't spoken for a long while? What if someone starts feeling nervous during a session or conversation—how could she let us know?

5. *No names:* Is it okay to talk about people who aren't in the group by name? Is it okay to use your name when someone refers to something you said in a previous session?

6. *Disagreement's okay, not judgment:* What's the difference between disagreeing and judging? Suggest the use of "I" statements; e.g., "In my opinion," "I think," "I feel," and so on. Is it okay for someone to give you feedback if you don't request it?

☞ *Teaching Note:* Point out that if you hear anything that suggests someone's health or life is in jeopardy, you will override the confidentiality ground rule and speak to whomever is needed to get help.

⊃ Invite girls to propose other ground rules. Write these in the space at the bottom of the sheet. Suggest an added guideline of your own: "We take positive action in the world every week." Emphasize that action is the key to success. Can everyone agree to this?

❧ Confidentiality Clause ❧

Parents will naturally ask their daughters about the group and get concerned if they respond, "It's confidential; I can't tell you anything." Many groups adopt a "home confidentiality" clause: It's okay to tell Mom or Dad *generally* what happened, topics discussed, or how you felt. Just don't share details or name names.

⊃ Ask the girls to gather around the newsprint with their partner from the previous activity. Each girl traces the outline of her partner's hand near the edge of the paper with a colored marker and then writes her partner's name in the center. Adult leaders participate, too. This group "handshake" forms a border around the ground rules.

⊃ Display the ground rules in a visible spot and ask the girls to read these aloud at the start of each session. At a certain point, perhaps halfway through the curriculum units, remove the rules from the wall and ask girls to recall them from memory. In this way, ground rules become internalized and, hopefully, carried beyond session walls.

⊃ Step in immediately whenever you note ground-rule violations, however minor.

Full of Ourselves: A Brainstorm

(Time Estimate: 10 minutes)

⊃ Kick off discussion with the following question:

" The title of this program is 'Full of Ourselves.' Let's figure out what it means to us. When you think about a girl or woman who is 'full of herself,' what words come to mind?"

⊃ *Prompts, if Necessary:* Can any of you think of a particular girl or woman who is "full of herself" (without naming names)? What's she like? How does she feel about herself? How do others view her?

⊃ List the girls' responses on the board, with negative takes in one column, positive takes in another.

☞ *Teaching Note:* Be sure to give credence to negative as well as positive impressions. Girls may strenuously resist seeing this phrase in any kind of positive light. This is okay and to be expected. In common parlance, the phrase connotes that someone is haughty or "full of it."

⊃ If girls offer *only* negative impressions, pull specifically for positives: "What's a more positive interpretation of this phrase?" Once girls offer even one positive word, ask them all to close their eyes and take a moment to remember a particular situation when they felt this way (e.g., "confident"). Then ask one girl to describe that situation and say more about how she felt in that moment. Add this description to the positive column.

⊃ It's important to give girls the chance to embody this discussion. This two-step process takes less than 1 minute to accomplish:

1. Ask one-half of the girls to stand up and show the group without speaking what the *negative take* on this phrase looks like: "In other words, let us *see* you look 'haughty' and 'stuck-up.'"
2. Ask the remaining girls to stand up and to show with their faces and bodies what the *positive take* on this phrase looks like: "Show us without speaking that you are self-confident and that you take yourself seriously."

⊃ Ask the girls to sit back down and summarize the new twist on the phrase offered by the program. Feel free to draw on the following script:

" You're all on target. In mainstream society, the phrase 'full of yourself' does have a negative meaning. But when we talk *here* about being 'full of yourself,' this doesn't mean being selfish or a snob or a bully. It doesn't mean that you know everything, that you always get your way, or that your life is perfect.

It *does* mean living powerfully and healthfully. It *does* mean being a girl leader. It *does* mean knowing that you can make a positive difference in the world in your own unique way—without stepping on others. You see, being 'full of yourself' doesn't mean being *only* for yourself. Instead, it means that you have a *strong sense of who you are* so you can be a more genuine friend, girlfriend, family member, and all-around citizen."

⊃ Hand out a "Full of Ourselves Proclamation" square to each girl (H-1A). Go around the circle, with each girl reading one of the points aloud. "A girl or woman who is full of herself—in the best sense of the phrase—might say things like . . ."

- I know who I am.
- I know that I matter.
- I know what matters to me.
- I pay attention to what I feel and what I need.
- I make choices and decisions that are good for me.
- I take good care of my body.
- I stand up for what I believe in.
- I let people know what I think, even when I'm angry or confused or in disagreement with everyone else.
- I am a valuable friend.
- I know I can make a positive difference in the world in my own unique way.

◐ Read the proclamation again in unison as a group. Discuss one or more of the following questions:

1. Look again at the list of proclamations. Check the statements that are true for you today. Which of these are true for you? Which ones aren't? Tell us about that.
2. Is it acceptable in this school for girls to be full of themselves in this new way—powerful, confident, and strong? If not, why not? How about in your family?
3. Is it acceptable in this school for boys to be strong and confident? Are there double standards for boys and girls? How come?
4. What kinds of things can make it hard to be strong and self-confident?

☞ *Teaching Note:* Sometimes girls' dislike of the program name threatens to preclude their enjoyment of the sessions. If this is the case with your

---

❖ Journal Note ❖

Journals are confidential. Girls can share these with each other or group leaders—if they choose. If girls consistently forget their journals, collect and keep them in a secure place between sessions. Invite girls to decorate the cover of their journals to "look like you": create a collage using pictures, poems, colors, words, and so on.

---

girls, don't force them to accept the program's positive reinterpretation of the phrase. Instead, invite girls to rename the group and "make it your own."

◐ Ask the girls to tape the squares onto the first page in their journals. Don't skip this step since you'll be referring girls back to the proclamation in later units.

Confidence and Power: A Freewrite
(Time Estimate: 5 minutes)

◐ Ask girls to write the following phrase at the top of a new page in their journals: "A time I felt really confident and powerful was . . ."

❝ Take two or three minutes to complete this sentence from your own experience. Be clear and honest! Write as much as you want and give details. You won't be handing this in."

◐ Ask two or three volunteers to read their sentence completion aloud. Ask each girl the following questions: How did you feel at that moment? How did you feel in your body?

◐ Point out that these are all examples of what it means to be "full of yourself" in the best sense of the phrase.

🕑 *Time Check:* If you have 10 extra minutes, after allowing for the "Body Scan" and "Call to Action," this is an ideal time to do the supplemental "Body Statues" activity.

Body Scan: A Guided Meditation
(Time Estimate: 5 minutes/3 minutes)

🕑 *Time Check:* If you're running short on time, eliminate the second paragraph of the meditation to save 2–3 minutes. Be sure to reserve time at the end of the session to review this week's "Call to Action."

Sample Lead-In:

❝ Our own bodies can be a source of power and confidence—*if* we take the time to stay connected to ourselves. This requires *awareness* . . . of our breathing, of our posture, of how we're feeling *right now* in this very moment. It's so easy to live 'in our heads' and to slip into body criticism and worries—worries about our hair or our noses or our legs—almost as if our bodies were something *other* than ourselves and other than a source of energy and life!

   We're going to try a body scan that will help to get us in touch ourselves and give us a deeper appreciation of our bodies as a source of power and life."

⊃ Ask girls to choose a comfortable place to lie down flat on their backs. If you're working with a co-leader, one of you should act as a role model and immediately lie down. Turn off the lights or close the shades to help everyone settle down.

⊃ Read the following script in a slow, gentle voice. Instruct girls to tune their attention inward and to follow your instructions without responding out loud. Pause for *5 seconds or more* at the end of each sentence. Literally count to 5 under your breath or on your fingers! In the suddenly quiet room, it's easy to speed up your reading. Resist this urge! It's better to err on the side of extended peace and quiet.

" Gently close your eyes and take a few long, smooth breaths . . . [5-second pause] . . . Let your body become very loose . . . [5-second pause] . . . Let your arms rest at your sides, palms facing up . . . Relax your shoulders . . . Let your feet fall out to the sides, relaxing your hips . . . As you breathe in, notice how your belly expands . . . As you exhale, notice how your belly sinks . . . Notice any sounds or movements in the room, and then gently bring your attention back to your breathing at your belly . . . Imagine you're lying on your own little island as you listen to my voice . . .

   Notice your body's temperature. Are you warm? Are you cool? . . . Notice your body's energy. Is it moving? Is it still? . . . Now gently bring your attention to your toes, without moving them if possible . . . Now notice your feet, the tops and bottoms . . . Notice your calves . . . your thighs . . . Notice the floor supporting your bottom . . . Now bring your attention to your tummy and the movement of your breath up and down . . . Now notice your chest and the pressure of your breath against your rib cage . . . Notice your lower back,

whether or not it's on the floor . . . your upper back . . . Notice your arms, your hands, and the tips of your 10 fingers . . . Feel the weight of your head resting on the ground . . . Feel the floor supporting your entire body . . .

   Now imagine that you are breathing through every pore of your skin. Feel every inhalation bringing positive, golden light into your body and mind . . . You soak up golden light like a sponge . . . It fills you with inner confidence and power . . . Notice the sensation of power and light throughout your entire body . . .

   Now gently bring your attention back to your breathing . . . Slowly deepen your breath . . . Wiggle your fingers and toes . . . Pretend you're a cat, and stretch your arms and legs in any way that feels comfortable to you . . . Bend your knees to your chest and roll to one side . . . Sit up slowly and notice how you feel."

⊃ Ask the girls to sit up and describe the body-scan experience and the sensations they noticed in their bodies: What did you notice? Did anything surprise you? Do you feel any differently now than when we started?

Call to Action Assignment
(Time Estimate: 5 minutes)

⊃ Reinforce the importance of action:

" We've covered a lot of ground today together in this group. But it will mean little if we don't put what we've learned into *practice* when we leave. In order for what we do here to have lasting meaning, we need to take *action*! This will be the real test of our success as individuals and as a group of girls."

⊃ Distribute the "Call to Action" handout (H-1B), review the assignment, and answer any questions.

⊃ Hold girls accountable. They'll be required to check in and report on their action steps at the beginning of the next session.

☞ *Teaching Note:* Decide beforehand how you will hold girls accountable for the action steps. Some

> ### ❀ Call to Action ❀
>
> These are required assignments, not optional! They go to the very heart of this work, asking girls to adopt leadership roles, to make positive choices, and to take definitive action on behalf of their own well-being. Action steps help determine the lasting success of each unit and of the program as a whole.

group leaders require written homework; for example, each girl submits a one-page written reflection on her experience with one of the action steps. Other group leaders forgo graded assignments in an attempt to distinguish this group from other academic classes. In either case, at the start of each session, require the girls to report verbally on their action steps.

Closing Circle
(Time Estimate: 15 seconds)

⊃ Tell the girls that you will end every group with a declaration of unity. Ask the girls to stand in a circle, join hands, and declare in unison: "We're in this together, differences included." If the girls dislike this statement, ask them to come up with one of their own.

SUPPLEMENTAL ACTIVITIES

Jumpstart: Catch!
(Time Estimate: 8 minutes)

⊃ This activity requires three balls that are made of a soft material; for example, stress-release balls, rolled-up socks, nerf balls, balled-up paper secured with masking tape, and so on.

⊃ Get the girls quickly involved:

" Let's play a game. I don't know some of you very well. Everybody up . . ."

⊃ Ask the girls to stand in a circle so that they can all see each other. Leaders are part of the circle, too.

Explain that this activity involves tossing a ball and that these are the rules:

1. The ball must be tossed underhand.
2. The purpose is to throw the ball so that it can be *caught*—in other words, stay in control!
3. We are going to create a "tossing pattern" so that everyone gets the ball before it returns to the first person.
4. Each girl gets/catches the ball just once.
5. The "tossing pattern" (order of tossing) will always be the same.

⊃ Say one of the girls' names and toss her a ball.

⊃ She says the name of another girl and tosses the ball to her. This keeps up until all the girls have been tossed the ball. The girls have now established the "tossing pattern."

⊃ Ask the girls to toss the ball around in the pattern 2–3 times, again saying aloud the name of the ball receiver before tossing her the ball.

⊃ Now add another ball: The girls are tossing two balls in the pattern.

⊃ Add a third ball so that three balls are being tossed around the circle at once. At some point the girls may have trouble keeping all the balls going; this is to be expected, along with much laughter and silliness. Give the girls several chances to try to keep all the balls going at once before interrupting the game to explain a new variable.

⊃ *New Variable:* Before you toss the ball, name one of your favorite foods. Name a different food each time the ball comes around to you. At first, the girls may struggle to think of foods. The list tends to get more detailed over time; for example, pomegranates, tuna sushi, green beans from my grandma's garden, and so on.

Body Statues
(Time Estimate: 10 minutes)

⊃ Clear a space big enough for the girls to move around in. If you have more than 10 girls, divide the group in half. One group will form the first statue while the second acts as "museum-goers." Girls switch roles for the second statue.

⟳ Introduce the activity:

" In a moment you are going to use your own bodies to create a group statue in this space. After I announce the title of the statue, take a minute to think about what this title means to you. At that point, any girl can enter the space and strike a pose relating to the title. Then, *one girl at a time*, others join in and add to the statue with a pose of your own."

⟳ Explain the three guidelines:

1. Build the statue without speaking a word.
2. When you join the statue, connect in at least one place; touch feet, arms, hands, and so on.
3. Try not to move.

⟳ Assign the title "Be a Good Girl" to the first statue and "Full of Ourselves" to the second. Once a statue is completed, ask the remaining girls to walk around it and comment on what they see. "If this statue could speak, what would it say? How do the people in this statue probably feel?"

Picture This: A Symbolic Drawing
(Time Estimate: 10 minutes)

⟳ Spread out crayons in the center of the circle. Ask girls to draw a picture in their journals symbolizing what it feels or looks like to be "full of yourself" in the best sense of the phrase. This may or may not be a self-portrait. Prompts, if necessary: What, to you, symbolizes fullness and strength? The sun? The color red?

⟳ Give girls the option of drawing with their "wrong" hand to relieve the pressure of creating an "accurate" representation.

Bioenergetic Punches
(Time Estimate: 10 minutes)

⟳ This activity gives girls and leaders alike the chance to tap into a physical sense of confidence and power. It is crucial that adult leaders wholeheartedly join in and demonstrate the punches.

⟳ Explain the activity:

" Everybody stand up. Let's practice standing up for ourselves and what we believe in. First, shake out your hands. Shake out your feet. Now jog in place for a minute to get some energy moving. Jog around the room if you feel like it . . .

Now stand in one place and feel yourself anchored to the ground. Imagine that there are roots growing out from the bottom of your feet. Ground your energy into the earth and feel the ground supporting you. Keep your knees bent so your energy doesn't get stuck or locked in your joints.

Now we're going to punch out into the air in front of us, one arm at a time. This isn't about learning how to fight. It's a *metaphor* for what it feels like to stand up for ourselves and to act powerfully in the world. "

⟳ Demonstrate for the girls and ask them to join you. Most girls and women have never been taught how to throw a proper punch. Here is a "punching primer," based on techniques drawn from self-defense programs:

- Stand with your feet planted firmly on the ground, one foot slightly in front of the other, shoulder-width apart.
- Keep your knees bent so that your energy doesn't get locked.
- Straighten your spine.
- Breathe deeply.
- Bend your elbows at a 90-degree angle to your waist.
- Form fists with your hands, thumbs remaining on the outside (so you don't break them).

" We contacted a local karate center and borrowed some karate punching squares for the girls to really hit away at."

—Adult leader, Bethel, Maine

- Punch out in front of you and hit your "target" with the top of your knuckles. Don't punch up or out to the sides.
- Shift your weight forward and back as you throw a punch to help you gain momentum.
- Guard your face with your opposite hand. Always be sure to protect your chin; it's the best place to land a knockout.

⊃ Punch gently at first, then gain in strength. Invite the girls to add voice to their punches. With each strong punch they might say, "Take that!"

⊃ As the girls punch, ask them to think about something or somebody that makes them really mad. Then ask them to imagine they are punching away evil in the world. Can they imagine themselves speaking and acting from a place as powerful as their punches every day?

☞ *Teaching Note:* Laughter and silliness are to be expected during this exercise. If the girls are hesitant to participate, ask them this question: "Imagine this was a group of guys. How would they respond to this activity?"

Unit Two: Claiming Our Strengths

ACTIVITIES

Core Activities
>   Action Check-In
>   Learning to Walk: Power of the Positive
>   Tree of Strength
>   Measuring Up: A Self-Assessment
>   Body Appreciation Relaxation
>   Call to Action Assignment
>   Closing Circle

Supplemental Activities
>   Freewrite: Making a Difference
>   Yoga Primer 1: Summoning Strength

UNIT OBJECTIVES

- To identify admirable qualities in oneself and others
- To learn the practice of positive self-talk (affirmations)
- To feel an embodied sense of strength

MATERIALS AND PREPARATION

- ☐ Supply a few healthy snacks, these should be easy-to-eat finger foods.
- ☐ Reminder: Handouts for all eight units can be found in Part Two.
- ☐ For the "Tree of Strength" activity, photocopy the "Tree of Strength" leaves (H-2A) and cut out two leaves per girl. Have hole punches, paper clips, markers, and masking tape on hand. Bring in a tree branch with many side branches. Prop up the branch in a coffee can filled with sand or rocks to hold it upright like a little tree. Girls will hang their leaves from this branch using paperclips. If a branch isn't handy, draw the outline of a tree on the board or newsprint onto which girls can tape their leaves.
- ☐ For the "Measuring Up" activity, write down the two self-assessment questions on a sheet of newsprint before the session. Keep from view until needed.
- ☐ Photocopy one "Call to Action" handout (H-2B) per girl.

CORE ACTIVITIES

Quick Ground-Rule Review

☑ *Reminder:* Post the ground rules so that everyone can see and read them aloud. Diligently follow and reinforce these rules, especially during the first few sessions.

Healthy Comment

⮌ As the group is settling in at the start, make a few short, seemingly off-the-cuff comments about the nutritional benefits of each snack. For example, "Cashews are loaded with protein, great for stamina. Snap peas contain lots of vitamin C to help you fight colds."

Action Check-in
(Time Estimate: 5–10 minutes)

☞ *Teaching Note:* This is a key moment of buy-in to the action component of the program! Take time to hold girls accountable for their action steps. Girls need to hear what others have done outside the group. Your response—especially to girls who resisted or dismissed the activity—makes a big difference. It's important not to chastise resistant girls; instead, investigate their resistance and encourage action from this point on.

Sample response:

" If you didn't take action, take a moment to ask yourself *why.* Was it hard taking time for yourself each day? Did the actions feel silly or awkward? If you don't give the action steps a try, it's kind of like you're devaluing yourself and your potential. It's hard to be powerful and healthy if you don't make the commitment to act on your ideals."

⮌ Let the girls know there won't be time to hear from everyone and that, at the start of each session, you will randomly call on girls to report on their actions. You expect everyone to be prepared to report.

✾ **Time Estimates** ✾

Rely on these as guidelines, not strictures. Some activities may go more quickly, others more slowly, with your group. While completing the unit is important, it's also vital to respect your girls, wherever they happen to be with the material, and give them space to explore relevant tangents off of a given topic. Use your discretion.

⮌ Call on different girls by name. If anyone reports that they didn't take action, ask them why not, as suggested above, and then solicit a response from someone else in the group: "Who else gave this action a try?"

- [Samantha], tell us about reading the proclamation every day. How did it sound to you over time? Can anyone recite it from memory?
- [Regina], did checking in with your body make a difference in your day?
- [Felicity], tell us about your first interview. Who did you talk to? When did she feel confident and powerful? What was your favorite part of the interview?
- [Kate], tell us about your second interview. When did a grown-up feel really proud of you? Were you surprised to hear this?
- [Harriet], tell us about a time you spoke your mind this week. How did it feel to stand up for yourself? Was it hard? How did you feel afterward? Were there any times you didn't speak up but wish you had?

⮌ Conclude with encouragement:

" This is a big deal! It's great that you all tried to put new ideas into practice. You took initiative. You exhibited leadership. This is how we change for the better—and change the world for the better—by taking simple steps every day. Over time, these add up to major breakthroughs."

Learning to Walk: Power of the Positive
(Time Estimate: 10 minutes)

⊃ Read aloud the following scenario:

" A little girl, an infant, is learning how to walk for the very first time. You are in the room with her, and she keeps falling down. Have any of you ever watched an infant do this? She lets go of a table leg and takes one or two steps—then boom!—down she goes."

⊃ Pose three questions:

1. What do you say to her?
2. Why don't you criticize her: "You're so stupid and uncoordinated! You can't do anything right!"
3. Which works better to help someone learn and grow: criticism or encouragement? How come?

⊃ Segue into the next phase of the activity:

" Our minds are extremely powerful. Just like it hurts when someone else says something mean to us, it hurts when we think or say negative things to ourselves. The opposite is true, too. Just like that little girl learning to walk, we change and grow when we feel validated and supported. Support can come from others, and it can also come from us! A great skill for getting through life is to learn the power of positive thinking. Did any of you read the children's book *The Little Engine That Could?* Can someone explain what that story's about?"

⊃ Read the directions, one step at a time. Allow the girls 1 minute to complete each step before moving on to the next:

1. Everyone close your eyes and take a deep breath. Now consider this question: What's an area in your life where you could use some encouragement? Think about a goal you want to reach in the next few days or weeks. Maybe you want to make a new friend, or land a babysitting job, or do better on your next math test. Scan your life and pinpoint something specific you'd like to achieve.
2. Open your eyes and write down your goal on a page in your journal.

❀ Quiet Girls ❀

Find out why they are quiet. If a girl hasn't spoken for a noticeable amount of time, check in with her privately after the session: "I noticed that you were quiet today. Is everything okay? Do you feel comfortable here?" Talk to other teachers to find out if this is typical behavior for this girl in other classrooms.

---

3. Underneath, write some words of encouragement to yourself. Try addressing yourself by name. "You can win that race, [Rachel], I know you can. I'm your biggest fan. Keep training!"
4. Now, write down three specific things you can do to move toward your goal.

⊃ Ask for volunteers to share their goal, encouragement, and action steps with the group.

Sample wrap-up:

" Keep in mind that little girl trying to walk. We all need encouragement to grow and to take positive action. As often as possible during the next few days, talk to yourself in the voice of a kind and supportive friend. In other words, try to be one of your own best friends!"

Tree of Strength
(Time Estimate: 15 minutes)

⊃ Tell girls they are going to construct a tree of strength:

" Another way to claim our own strengths is by looking to women for inspiration."

" Preserve your tree of strength! We drew a tree on newsprint and then taped on the completed leaves. The girls liked it so much we decided to get it laminated, something we couldn't have done if we'd used a tree branch."

—Adult leader, Deerfield, New Hampshire

⊃ Ask each girl to list in her journal the names of five women she thinks are admirable and powerful in some way:

" Write down the names of five women you admire, women who are special to you and who have somehow had an impact on your life. They don't have to be 'famous' in the traditional sense of the word."

⊃ Women can include relatives, ancestors, friends, neighbors, women in history, or fictional characters. One guideline: No movie stars or TV characters.

⊃ Next to each woman's name, ask girls to write down one or two traits that they admire in that woman and hope to emulate.

⊃ Hand out one Tree of Strength leaf to each girl (H-2A). Ask the girls to choose one woman to "introduce" to the group and to write her name in the center of the leaf.

⊃ Have a Tree of Strength ceremony. Each girl stands up and introduces her woman to the group. She then punches a hole in the leaf and hangs it on a tree branch using an opened paperclip.

⊃ Point out that these women are examples of what it means to be "full of yourself" in the best sense of the phrase.

Measuring Up: A Self-Assessment
(Time Estimate: 10 minutes)

⊃ Introduce the activity:

" Now let's congratulate ourselves for who we are today and add our names to the tree of strength."

⊃ Read the following questions, one at a time, allowing 1–2 minutes between each question for the girls to write down answers in their journals.

" The traits girls shared were impressive. They admired perseverance, determination, kindness, and stability."

—Adult leader, Greenwich, Connecticut

1. What do you (perhaps secretly or privately) really like about yourself? Prompts: Are you a good sister? Do you help friends through rough times? Do you have a great singing voice? Do you take your spiritual side seriously?
2. What would you like other people to appreciate about you more often?

☞ *Teaching Note:* Encourage girls to focus on talents, actions, or aspects of their characters or personalities, rather than physical traits.

⊃ Go around the circle, asking each girl to read at least one answer from her list. If anyone had a hard time thinking of an answer, ask group members to name something positive about her.

⊃ On the second leaf cutout (H-2A), ask girls to write their own name and add this to the Tree of Strength. Display the tree in a prominent place.

⊃ Some girls may find it difficult to "brag" about themselves. Whether or not this is the case, offer the following insight:

" Sometimes it's hard to applaud ourselves. But I want you to consider this: It's only by keeping in touch with our strengths that we can make a positive difference in the world. Remember:

- Liking yourself is not the same as being selfish.
- Respecting yourself is not the same as being stuck-up.
- Standing up for yourself is not the same as being pushy.
- Taking yourself seriously does not mean you are too intense.
- Telling the truth doesn't mean you're too loud or that you talk too much.
- Being in touch with your heart is not the same as being too emotional."

Body Appreciation Relaxation
(Time Estimate: 5 minutes)

⊃ Segue into the relaxation:

" Here's another secret you might not know: In order to be a leader, you can't get caught up in hating or criticizing your body. This will instantly derail you from being a healthy and powerful person."

⊃ Are the girls aware that in both Native American and Orthodox Judaism religious traditions there are specific prayers for every part of the body—even prayers of gratitude for the ability to poop and pee?

⊃ Explain that the group is going to try a guided meditation that will help everyone get in touch with the miracle of their own bodies. Ask the girls to find a spot on the floor and to lie down on their backs. Then read the meditation in a calm voice, pausing for 5 seconds or more at the end of each instruction:

" Close your eyes, if you feel comfortable doing so, and take a few deep breaths . . . [pause] . . . When you breathe in, let your belly expand and contract . . . [pause] . . . Notice what other parts of your body move as you breathe . . . Notice your body being supported by the floor . . . Allow all your muscles to release and sink into the floor . . . Notice any sounds in the room, and then bring your attention back to your breathing at your belly . . . Notice your thoughts and let them wash away like leaves in a stream . . . Notice how you are feeling . . . Perhaps calm and peaceful, or maybe anxious or sad . . . Allow any feelings to wash away with your breaths . . .

Now focus your attention on your breath traveling down into your lungs. Imagine your lungs being surrounded with soft white light, and appreciate the work they do to bring oxygen into your bloodstream . . .

Now sense your breath flowing directly into your heart, a muscle that pumps nourishing blood to every inch of your body . . .

Now breathe into your belly where your stomach digests food to give you energy to live and run and think . . .

Now sense your breath traveling down your spine, one vertebra at a time . . . Surround your backbone with light and appreciate how your spine supports you in all your movements . . .

Imagine your breath traveling into your hips and pelvic area. Breathe white light to your ovaries and your uterus, and be grateful for all your creative energies, including the capacity to create life inside you . . .

Breathe now into your thighs, into your calves, all the way down your legs to your feet and the tips of your toes. Appreciate all the places your legs and feet carry you and will carry you throughout your life . . .

Breathe beautiful light down your arms to your hands and fingertips. Appreciate your capacity to touch and be touched . . .

Now breathe gently into your neck and up into your head and your skull, which protects your amazing human mind . . .

Imagine the organ of your brain shrinking inside your skull, creating more space. Let any thoughts drift by like clouds through the sky . . .

Now gently consider this question and answer it quietly to yourself: What do you most appreciate about your body right now . . . ?

Now slowly and gently bring yourself back . . . Deepen your breath . . . Wiggle your fingers and toes . . . Become aware of the floor underneath you and how it is supporting your body. Notice the sounds in the room. Stretch your arms and legs in any way that feels comfortable to you . . . When you are ready, open your eyes."

⊃ Ask girls to describe the experience:

1. What sorts of things did you notice during the relaxation?
2. Do you feel any differently than when we started?
3. What did you appreciate about your body?

Call to Action Assignment
(Time Estimate: 5 minutes)

⊃ Distribute "Call to Action" (H-2B) and review the assignments:

" We've covered a lot of ground today together in this group. Now let's carry what we've learned out into our lives."

⊃ Answer any questions, and remind girls they'll be required to report on action steps at the start of the next session.

Closing Circle
(Time Estimate: 15 seconds)

⟳ Stand in a circle. Ask everyone to join hands and affirm in unison: "We're in this together, differences included."

☞ *Teaching Note:* It can take time to establish a sense of trust both among girls and among girls and adult leaders. This is one reason sessions end with a statement of unity and purpose.

SUPPLEMENTAL ACTIVITIES

Freewrite: Making a Difference
(Time Estimate: 10 minutes)

⟳ Introduce the activity:

" Freewrites are a way for us to get in touch with what we really think and feel. This writing is for you alone. No one has to share their writing unless they want to. Let's see what it might look like—and feel like—to be a powerful leader in the world. Everyone close your eyes, if you feel comfortable doing so, and imagine yourself 15 years from now. Imagine that you are an influential woman in her mid-20s. What are you doing? What kinds of contributions are you making to the world around you?"

⟳ Ask everyone to take a few deep breaths and collect their thoughts. Write the following prompt on the board or a sheet of newsprint: (Your full name), at age 25, has just been elected Young Woman of the Year . . .

" This is the title of a newspaper article. Write about what you hope your remarkable accomplishments will be. Pretend someone else—a reporter—is writing the article. Write from their point of view in the third-person voice."

⟳ Allow the girls 5 minutes for personal writing. Adult leaders should participate in this activity, too (add a decade to your present age).

⟳ Ask for volunteers to read their freewrites aloud.

Yoga Primer 1: Summoning Strength
(Time Estimate: 20 minutes)

⟳ Invite girls to try some simple yoga postures as a way to connect to inner soundness and strength.

⟳ Turn to the "Yoga Primer" (Addendum A) and advance through the first sequence of discussion and postures:

Introduction and Warm-Up Questions
Energetic Warm-Up: Arm Swing
Warrior 1
Child Pose
Debriefing

Unit Three: Body Politics

ACTIVITIES

Core Activities
Action Check-In
Changing Bodies, Changing Lives
Dear Body: Note of Appreciation
Imagine That Woman: A Discussion
Fat Myths
Group Pledge
Call to Action Assignment
Closing Circle

Supplemental Activities
The Human Knot
Dear Body: A Response

OBJECTIVES

- To encourage candid talk about ways bodies change during adolescence
- To identify weightism as a form of prejudice
- To dispel common myths about body fat
- To begin the actual practice of body-size tolerance

MATERIALS AND PREPARATION

- ☐ Provide healthy snacks and beverages.
- ☐ For the "Fat Myths" activity, make "Agree" and "Disagree" signs.
- ☐ Photocopy "Fat Myths" (H-3A), cut into strips, and place in a paper bag.
- ☐ Review the "Fat Myths: Answer Guide for Adult Leaders" at the end of this unit.
- ☐ Photocopy "Group Pledge" (H-3B) and cut out one square per girl.
- ☐ Photocopy one "Call to Action" handout (H-3C) per girl.

CORE ACTIVITIES

Ground-Rule Review

⊃ Keep this short: "Let's quickly review our ground rules without looking at the list. What did we decide to do to make this the best group possible?"

Healthy Comment

⊃ As girls settle in, make casual comments about the nutritional benefits of each snack. For example, "Pecans are great for your skin, loaded with protein and vitamin E. Strawberries are stress busters, packed with vitamin C."

Action Check-In

(Time Estimate: 10 minutes)

⊃ Call on girls to report. Choose different girls from the prior session.

- What was your affirmation? Did you repeat it every day? What effect did this have?
- What made it onto your gratitude list?
- Whom did you interview? Whom did they admire?
- Did you talk with one of your powerful women? How did she respond? Was she surprised to hear from you?
- Did any of you stand up for yourself, for someone else, or for something you believe in?

🕐 *Time Check:* If time permits, do the 5-minute supplemental "Human Knot" activity at this point.

❧ Girl Leadership ❧

At the end of the Full of Ourselves units, group members will lead sessions with younger girls. Whenever possible, let girls take the lead. Have them read handouts, talk from their own experiences, debrief the "Call to Action" assignments, and so on. Rotate leadership opportunities among all girls.

It's beneficial to get girls up and moving before the "Changing Bodies" brainstorm. Don't skip unless you're really short on time!

Changing Bodies, Changing Lives

(Time Estimate: 10 minutes)

⊃ Sit in a circle for a group brainstorm and explain the activity:

1. The goal is to get down as many ideas on the sheet of newsprint as possible.
2. No one has to agree, and no idea is too silly or personal to say.

⊃ Ask the girls to close their eyes and imagine themselves back in the 4th grade:

" Close your eyes and put yourself in your own 8-year-old shoes. What do you look like in 4th grade? How do you wear your hair? What clothes are you wearing? How does it feel to be you, walking around in your 8-year-old body?"

⊃ Ask girls to open their eyes:

" Imagine this: You are all asked to be on a panel of middle school girls who will talk to a group of 4th-grade girls about what it's like to go through adolescence. The topic of the panel discussion is: 'Ways My Body Has Changed Since 4th Grade.' What are some of the things you'd tell the younger girls?"

⊃ Pose questions to help organize the brainstorm and keep girls on track:

1. What was your body like when you were in 4th grade?
2. How has your body changed between then and now? Prompt girls, if needed:

   - How about height? Have any of you grown taller?
   - What about weight?
   - How about hair? Where do you notice new hair?
   - How about sweat?
   - How about baby fat?
   - What about cramps? PMS? (*Note:* These words are better than "periods.")

❧ Judgment Call ❧

If girls make critical remarks about their 4th-grade selves, name what you are hearing: "I'm hearing some judgmental remarks. Was the 4th grader critical of herself or is that *you* now?" Remind girls of the importance of positive self-talk: "Just like it hurts when someone else criticizes us, we hurt ourselves when we judge ourselves." Ask girls to open their journals and write a few words of encouragement to their younger selves.

- What about getting your first bra?
- What about skin?

3. Are there any changes you are still waiting for?
4. What is an embarrassing or awkward "body moment" you've had in the past few years?
5. What is something about your body that you feel good about today—other than appearance? Prompts, if needed: energy level, skills, strengths, stamina, and so on.

⊃ Conclude with two points:

1. Agree or disagree: Between the ages of 8 and 14, girls gain an average of 40 pounds.

❝ This is true! A 40-pound weight gain over 5 years is healthy and normal. Everyone's growth spurt is different, of course. Some girls get chubbier before their height catches up; other girls shoot up 6 inches or more before the rest of their body fills out. The point is, you are all in a growing stage of life and need to gain weight to be strong and healthy. Of course, if you gain weight too rapidly, 20–40 pounds in 6 months or 1 year, something else might be going on. You might not be eating in a healthy way, or you might have a medical problem that needs to get checked out."

2. Point out that bodies continue to change throughout our entire lives; speak from your own experience as a woman—as is appropriate and as you are comfortable.

Dear Body: A Note of Appreciation
(Time Estimate: 5 minutes)

⊃ Girls work in their journals. Ask everyone to take a few deep breaths before starting to write. Explain that this writing is personal and does not have to be shared.

⊃ *Dear Body, . . .* Write this prompt on the board and ask girls to write at least five sentences of appreciation to their bodies. Each sentence begins with the phrase: "Thank you for . . ." Their notes can also contain questions they'd like their bodies to answer.

⊃ Adult leaders should participate, too; it's useful for girls to see you taking the activity seriously—although, in the case of freewrites, it's best not to share your writing aloud.

⊃ Ask for volunteers to share with the group. Be careful not to critique or comment directly on the writing. Instead, invite other girls into the conversation by asking questions such as these: Has anyone else ever felt this way? Did anyone write something similar? Did anyone write something different?

🕐 *Time Check:* If time allows, try the 10-minute supplemental "Dear Body: A Response" activity.

Imagine That Woman: A Discussion
(Time Estimate: 10 minutes)

⊃ Introduce the discussion:

❝ People tend to have a lot of different opinions about bodies—especially about bodies of different shapes and sizes. Many of these opinions are stereotypes. Can somebody explain what 'stereotyping' is?"

We're going to take an up-close and personal look at a stereotype we all live with, although we're not always aware of the ways it affects and limits us. I'm going to describe two people, and I want you to imagine them in your minds. I'm going to ask what you might think about these two people based just on what I tell you about them.

I'd like us all to be honest—even though we might feel pretty uncomfortable about some of the things we think."

> " Whenever possible, build in 20-minute segments for discussion to fully unfold."
> —Adult leader, Deerfield, New Hampshire

⊃ Give girls permission to use whatever language they want; decide beforehand whether or not profanity is permissible.

⊃ Write the heading "Woman 1" on top of a sheet of newsprint and the heading "Woman 2" on top of a second sheet. Then lead off a discussion by describing the following hypothetical situation. Write down the girls' answers, documenting "positive" associations on the left-hand side of the page, "negative" ones on the right.

" Imagine that you see a woman walking down the street who is really beautiful by society's standards. She has a great body, she's stylishly dressed—whatever that looks like to you. What do you think her life is like? Just by looking at her, what might you assume?"

⊃ Pose the following questions in quick succession. Probe for negative assumptions as well as positive ones. Encourage the girls to be honest and spontaneous: "You can say whatever you want—what you really think. We don't all have to agree."

- Does she have friends?
- What kind of job do you think she might have?
- Do you think she's in a relationship?
- Does she have children?
- Is she educated?
- Is she happy?

- Where does she live? What's her home like?
- If you saw her on the street, where might you imagine she is going?
- How does *she* feel about herself?
- How do *you* feel about her?
- Put yourself in this woman's shoes. Would any of you want to be Woman 1?

☞ *Teaching Note:* The girls' answers may seem mutually exclusive; for example, they may describe Woman 1 as "an airhead" *and* as someone with "a high-powered job." This is fine; the point of the activity is to probe for as many assumptions as possible.

⊃ Pose a second hypothetical question about Woman 2 and record the girls' answers in a similar manner on the second sheet of newsprint.

" In your mind, imagine a woman who looks like the opposite of Woman 1. She's unattractive by society's standards, perhaps she has a bigger body—whatever that looks like to you. What do you think or assume about her—what is she like, and what is her life like?"

⊃ Again pull for a range of assumptions, both negative and positive. Assure girls that they can have different opinions. Encourage honesty: "Pretend you are right there seeing her walk down [Main Street]. What would you *really* think?"

☞ *Teaching Note:* If the girls start to chastise each other for being mean, step in and assure them that every assumption is permissible in this activity and that, while we don't like to admit it, we all make snap judgments sometimes.

Example:

Woman 1		Woman 2	
(+)	(-)	(+)	(-)
great job	airhead/ditz	good friend	poor
perfect life	stuck up	nurturer	fat
perfect husband	spoiled	nice	lonely
happy children	works out all day	good with animals	stupid
good college			lazy
happy, likes herself			depressed
loved			troubled
in control			no control
successful			day-care worker
(how do you feel about her)		*(how do you feel about her)*	
jealous		pity her	
hate her		scared of her	

☞ *Teaching Note:* The way you debrief this activity is crucial. By all means, do not judge girls for making judgments about the two women—that was the objective of the exercise. Instead, help girls understand why it's so easy for everyone to make snap judgments about others based solely on their body size, shape, and appearance.

⤳ Segue into discussion:

" Look at all the assumptions all of us make. Wow! How did we get here?! Isn't it weird how easy this was for us to do?"

⤳ Discussion questions:

1. Where do we get these ideas? It's not by accident that most people make judgments based on body size and shape. From an early age, we're bombarded with messages that teach us how to make snap judgments.
2. Can someone explain what racism is?
3. Who can explain what sexism is?
4. Now, who can guess what weightism is?

⤳ Write the term "Weightism" on the board. This script introduces a key program concept. Do not skip!

" We all know how cruel racism is—it's really serious, unfair, and hurtful to judge someone because of the color of his or her body. It's also really serious, unfair, and hurtful to judge a person based on the shape or size of his or her body. This is called 'weightism.' Weightism is a form of prejudice, just like racism. It's a set of beliefs and attitudes that says someone is better or smarter or more beautiful just because of the shape and size of her body.

In mainstream White culture here in America, weightism says that thinness is ideal and that chubby bodies and weight gain are bad. In other cultures, rounder and fuller bodies are considered ideal.

Either way, whether a girl's put down or put up on a pedestal just because she's heavy or just because she's thin, it's unfair. Judgments are being made based on what she looks like on the outside without knowing who she is inside: her personality; her spirit; her talents; her interests; what she thinks

about, cares about, worries about, dreams about; and how she makes the world a better place.

Have you ever noticed weightism in your own lives?"

Fat Myths
(Time Estimate: 10 minutes)

⤳ Make "Agree" and "Disagree" signs and post these on opposite sides of the room. Cut the four "Fat Myths" (H-3A) into strips and put them in a paper bag.

☞ *Teaching Note:* Set a fast pace for this activity. After the previous discussion, the girls will enjoy the energizing movement. No lengthy discussions are necessary here, just quick exchanges of information.

⤳ Ask the girls to think again about Woman 2, the overweight woman, and how easy it is to make assumptions about people based solely on their looks. Then ask for a volunteer to pull a statement from the paper bag and read it to the group. The girls should listen carefully to the statement, decide whether or not they agree, and stand under the corresponding sign. "Undecided" girls can sit on the fence in the middle of the room.

⤳ Ask the girls to talk briefly with other members of their opinion group: "See if you have the same reasons for being in your spot."

⤳ After a minute or two, ask one spokesperson from each group to explain their reasoning. If all the girls take the same position, play devil's advocate to make sure their reasoning is strong. Supplement the girls' explanations and debunk the myth with information from the "Fat Myths: Answer Guide for Adult Leaders."

⤳ Repeat this exercise with the remaining statements.

⤳ To conclude, explain that you'll have in-depth discussions about how to live healthfully in following sessions. The point of this exercise was to debunk some of the most common myths about overweight people like Woman 2.

Group Pledge
(Time Estimate: 3 minutes)

❝ One thing we can agree to start doing right now is to try not to judge or tease other people—or ourselves—for how we look.❞

⟳ Hand out copies of the "Group Pledge" (H-3B). Give girls a few seconds to read silently to themselves. Can everyone agree to this? If so, ask girls to read the pledge aloud in unison.

⟳ Instruct girls to tape the pledge to the top of a journal page and then to sign their names underneath. If time allows, invite girls to hand their journals around the circle to give everyone the chance to sign their names to the group pledge.

Call to Action Assignment
(Time Estimate: 5 minutes)

⟳ Reinforce the importance of "walking the talk":

❝ We've covered a lot of ground today. Now the challenge is to walk the talk outside the group! Let's take a look at this week's Call to Action.❞

⟳ Hand out "Call to Action" sheets (H-3C) and review the assignments. Introduce the third section, "Action in the World," like this:

❝ You are the experts of your world. You know how your friends and family members talk and act. You watch TV and listen to music. You know what's inside magazines geared toward girls your age. So you're in a great position to be social scientists.❞

⟳ Answer any questions. Tell girls you look forward to hearing about their action steps at the start of the next session.

Closing Circle
(Time Estimate: 15 seconds)

⟳ Stand in a circle. Ask everyone to join hands. Affirm in unison: "We're in this together, differences included."

SUPPLEMENTAL ACTIVITIES

The Human Knot
(Time Estimate: 5 minutes)

⟳ You need an even number of people; one of the leaders can join in if there is an odd number of girls in your group.

⟳ Explain the directions:

❝ Everyone stand in a circle, shoulder to shoulder, and close your eyes. Reach your right hand into the circle and grab another person's hand—but not your immediate neighbor's.

1. Now reach your left hand into the circle and take hold of a free left hand.
2. Open your eyes and try to untangle yourselves. You can talk with one another, change grips, and climb over or under one another's arms, but do not release anyone's hand.❞

☞ *Teaching Note:* In some cases the human knot cannot be completely unwoven. This is okay, as the point of the exercise is to encourage teamwork and communication among the girls.

⟳ Debriefing questions:

1. What helped most to unravel the knot?
2. In what ways is this activity like life itself?

Dear Body: A Response
(Time Estimate: 10 minutes)

☞ *Teaching Note:* This activity should follow directly on the heels of "Dear Body: A Note of Appreciation" in the Core Activities section.

⟳ Dear [your own name], . . . Write this prompt on the board. Girls are now to write a note back to themselves from their bodies.

❝ What does your body have to say to you in response to your note and your questions? Close your eyes and tune your attention inward. If your body could speak, what would it say?❞

⊃ Suggest that girls try writing with their "wrong" hand to help them snap out of their accustomed way of thinking.

⊃ Ask for volunteers to share their writing with the group. Invite other girls into the conversation by asking questions like these: Has anyone else ever felt like this? Did anyone write something similar? Did anyone write something different?

BACKGROUND NOTES

Fat Myths: Answer Guide for Adult Leaders

Body fat is bad; it serves no good purpose on anybody's body.

A myth. A certain amount of body fat is crucial to your health. Body fat insulates you from the cold. It cushions your bones and inner organs against shock. And it stores energy so you can dance and run and move whenever you want. Girls, especially, need to put on extra body fat during puberty. This is normal, healthy, and necessary! The added fat helps support your ability to menstruate and get ready to bear children.

While having too little body fat is unhealthy, the same goes for having too much. There are serious health issues related to having too much body fat. Luckily, your brain comes wired with a thermostat that knows how much body fat you actually need. If you eat healthy food in healthy amounts, your body will stay in a healthy range and know how much fat you need.

The thinnest girl in the room is the happiest girl in the room.

This is the myth that all advertisers want us to believe: The thinnest girl, or the prettiest girl, is the guaranteed happiest girl. And that if we buy products to change our appearance on the outside, we'll magically feel better on the inside. But someone's body size or appearance does not give any clue to their emotional, spiritual, or mental well-being. Thin people have worries, fears, and problems just like anyone else. Many heavy people are happy, healthy, and leading fulfilling lives. You can't tell about someone's inside by simply looking at their outside.

People get fat because they eat too much and exercise too little.

Sometimes this is true, sometimes it's not. How much you eat and exercise certainly plays a part in determining your weight and body shape. Some people gain unneeded weight because they eat too much food, choose foods that are high in fats and sugars, and don't exercise enough. Our society doesn't help much—we are surrounded by fast-food restaurants that offer supersizes, and technological advances such as cars, televisions, and computers make it easy to be less active. But there's more to the story. Consider these factors:

1. Heredity and genetics are a big influence on body size: Humans are designed to come in all shapes and sizes. Some people exercise regularly and eat healthfully and their bodies are just naturally heavier than others'.

2. Other people put on extra weight because they overeat to try to cope with underlying problems. Food can be a source of comfort (comfort foods) in the short term, but food can't take away your problems. This is a common way people put on unneeded weight.

3. Other people have gone on and off so many diets, their bodies have gotten totally confused. This is called "yo-yo dieting." When you go on and off a lot of diets, the messages get scrambled between your brain and body telling you when you're hungry and when you've had enough to eat. Thus, dieting can actually lead to eating more and gaining weight. If someone needs to lose

weight, the best thing to do is to avoid fad diets and focus on long-term changes in eating and activity behaviors.

The thinner you are, the healthier you are.

Not always; it depends on the individual. Being thin doesn't necessarily mean someone's healthy, or flexible, or resistant to illness. Thin people might not exercise or eat nutritiously. Or they might be exercising way too much and taxing their body. Or they may be very healthy and genetically programmed to be thin.

The same goes for heavier people. They can be big-boned *and* exceptionally fit, healthy, and strong; they're just genetically programmed to be on the larger side. Other people, if they don't exercise enough or eat too much junk food, gain unneeded weight that's unhealthy for their bodies and leads to health problems. The point is, you can't tell about people's health simply by looking at their bodies. It's impossible to make generalizations.

Unit Four:
Standing Our Ground

ACTIVITIES

Core Activities
- Action Check-In
- The Comeback Kid: Assertiveness Training
- The Cafeteria: Bullies and Bystanders
- The Party: A Role Play
- The Wall: A Role Play
- One-Minute Body Scan
- Call to Action Assignment
- Closing Circle

Supplemental Activities
- Guest Leader
- Yoga Primer 2: Standing Ground
- Getting to Know You: Interviews
- Original Role Plays
- Comic Strips

OBJECTIVES

- To practice standing up for oneself and others
- To put oneself in the shoes of people involved in weightist incidents: bullies, targets, bystanders, followers, and activists
- To understand the courage required to be an activist who intervenes on someone else's behalf

MATERIALS AND PREPARATION

- ☐ Provide healthy snacks and beverages.
- ☐ For the "Comeback Kid" activity, photocopy the "Quick Comebacks" (H-4A) and cut into separate scripts. Each girl gets one copy of each of the three scripts.
- ☐ Make a single copy of "The Cafeteria" (H-4B).
- ☐ For "The Party" role play, write out nametags for each character, including the narrator. Make four copies of "The Party" (H-4C), one for each of the characters and the narrator. To make it easier for actors to track their lines, highlight on each copy the name of a given character throughout the scene. Photocopy "The Party: Assigned Roles" (H-4D), and cut out one square for each remaining girl not involved in the role play.
- ☐ Photocopy five copies of "The Wall" (H-4E).
- ☐ Photocopy one "Call to Action" handout (H-4F) per girl.

CORE ACTIVITIES

Ground-Rule Review

☑ *Reminder:* Post the rules so that everyone can see. Ask girls to read them aloud.

Healthy Comment

⮑ As girls settle in, make casual comments about the nutritional benefits of each snack. For example, "Apricots contain lots of vitamin C to help you fight colds. If you find yourself needing energy to stay alert, try snacking on some sunflower seeds, packed with iron."

Action Check-In
(Time Estimate: 10 minutes)

⮑ Call on individual girls to report on each action. Choose a different set of girls from the prior session.

1. Can you recite the group pledge for us? Can you think of a time you put it into action during the week?
2. Whom did you interview and what did she tell you?

⮑ Spend the bulk of your time debriefing the "social scientist" action. This consciousness-raising activity is central to the program, giving girls the chance to relate new ideas to their own experience.

⮑ Ask two or three girls to report their observations, reminding them of the ground rule discouraging the use of real names. Decide beforehand whether or not it's okay for girls to report offensive terms. One point of the activity is to get an accurate picture of weightism, which, by definition, causes offense and discomfort.

⮑ If girls cite examples from primarily one source (e.g., TV), prompt them to broaden their investigation: Did you overhear anything in the lunchroom? Anyone hear an adult make a body comment—positive, negative, or merely descriptive? What about boys?

> ### ❀ Phase 2: Throw Your Weight Around ❀
>
> If you haven't done so by now, start to plan for phase 2 of the program. Make contact with the leader of younger girls, set dates, arrange transportation, and so on. During group meetings, pause every so often and ask the girls questions like these: How would you get this idea across to a bunch of 4th graders? What would you say or do to get them to understand this idea?

⮑ Ask girls how the comments/incidents made them feel: How did you feel when you heard/saw that? What could you do or say in response if you heard/saw this again tomorrow?

⮑ *Interesting Note:* According to many girls, a positive comment from a parent "doesn't count."

⮑ Examples overheard by a group of 6th-grade girls.

(+)
beautiful hands
prettiest smile
gorgeous eyes
nice "stems"
perky bottom
nice teeth

(-)
flat as a fritter
you're fat
mini-muffins
whistle on street
sick cow
ugly dog
you're a "big" girl

(+/-)
you look like Britney Spears
you're so skinny

⟡ **Dealing with Digressions** ⟡

When girls diverge from one topic to another, point out the digression and ask them to draw connections between two topics: "Can anyone figure out what B has to do with A?" If topic B will be explored in a later session, let the girls know and reaffirm the connections to the topic at hand before continuing.

⊃ Discussion questions (see following "Notes" for debriefing pointers):

1. Who makes the most body comments about *themselves*, males or females? How come?

2. Who makes more body comments about *others*, males or females? Are these comments most often negative, positive, or neutral?

3. Imagine this: A 4-year-old girl sees an overweight man on the street and says, "Mommy, he's *fat*!" Is this "bad body talk"? Is "fat" a weightist word?

4. Imagine this: An older boy says something mean about the way you look. You don't like what he says and don't really believe him, either. But he's a very popular boy in the grade ahead of you. How do you *not* take on his comment? How do you hold on to what *you* think about yourself?

⊃ *Note 1:* In some cases a girl will insist that derogatory body comments are okay as long as they come from a friend. For example, "My girlfriend calls me big butt and that's fine with me. We're friends." In this instance, it's best not to argue to the contrary, but instead to ask, "What if a *boy* or a *stranger* said that to you?"

⊃ *Note 2:* Is the word "fat" weightist? It depends. Sometimes the word "fat" is cruel and prejudicial; other times it's merely a descriptive term without pejorative meaning. An overweight girl can be described as "fat," as she might also be described as "freckled" or "tall," without making related (weightist) assumptions about her intelligence, character, and so on. Similarly, a Jewish or African-American girl can be described as "a Jew" or "a Black" without making anti-Semitic or racist assumptions about her intelligence, character, class background, eating habits, and so on. In another instance this same girl might be cruelly teased and harassed simply *because* she is "fat," "a Jew," or "a Black." When a term is used with the *intention* of shaming, hurting, or humiliating, it is not merely descriptive; it is mean and prejudicial. Tone of voice is often a giveaway.

⊃ *Note 3:* Girls may offer examples of behavior and comments that could be classified as sexual harassment (i.e., unwanted, unwelcomed, frightening, demeaning). Point out that sexual harassment makes it very hard to accept one's body. And let girls know that sexual harassment should not be tolerated in schools—it's illegal. Your school is required by law to have a sexual harassment policy. If any girl feels she's being sexually harassed by a student or an adult at school, she should go immediately to a school counselor, administrator, or other trusted adult; tell them about the situation; and ask for help. Offer to accompany her.

⊃ Reinforce the importance of awareness:

" This is a big deal! You took initiative. You opened your eyes and have begun to notice—and name—a form of social injustice. With raised awareness, you're now in a great position to begin standing your ground, speaking up, and changing things for the better. That's what we're going to practice doing today. As social scientists we're keeping an eye out for bad body comments and behaviors. The next step is to become activists and take action to eliminate weightism altogether."

The Comeback Kid: Assertiveness Training
(Time Estimate: 10 minutes)

⊃ Get girls quickly up and moving. Progress from one scene right into the next. Note that the "assertiveness degree of difficulty" increases with each scene.

⊃ Prompt discussion by asking if anyone's familiar with Rosa Parks. What do you know about her? Can

> ### ❧ "I" Statements ❧
>
> Keep an ear out for advice-giving and broad generalizations. Girls may resort to these in an attempt to distance themselves from difficult topics. These tendencies, while natural, can disrupt group cohesion. When you hear a girl giving advice, however well meaning, or talking about the opinions of "all girls," interrupt and ask her to try to speak from her own experience using the first-person pronoun "I." By doing so, she takes full responsibility for herself and her words carry much more authority.

anyone figure out what she might have to do with a discussion of weightism?

" Because of the color of her skin, Rosa Parks was told she couldn't do certain things. But look what she did! She didn't accept the rules; she summoned her courage and took action. Of course, she was well trained and practiced in civil disobedience. She was part of a larger civil rights movement.

It also takes courage and training to fight mean and prejudiced messages about the shapes of our bodies. And in order to take a stand, you need to be *self-possessed*."

⊃ Write the following statement on the board: *She is self-possessed.* Is this a positive or negative thing to say about someone? Prompt, if necessary: What's a possession?

" A possession is something you own, something that belongs to you. If a girl is self-possessed, she belongs to *herself.* She has power over her own attitudes, actions, and decisions. In other words, she doesn't let other people—or images in magazines or peer pressure—define her. She's self-confident. Let's see what self-possession feels like."

⊃ Girls work in pairs. If needed, you can pair with an odd-numbered girl.

⊃ Hand out a copy of "Comeback 1: Shoes" (H-4A) to each pair. Explain that it's often easier to be asser-

tive on behalf of a possession than it is to stand up for ourselves.

⊃ Explain the directions:

1. One person in each pair takes off one of her shoes and holds it in her hand. She is the target. (Roles switch later.)
2. The harasser walks up to the target, grabs for the shoe, and aggressively reads her line: "I want that shoe! Give it to me!"
3. The target responds with her "comeback" in a strong assertive voice. Point out that this doesn't necessarily mean a *loud* voice. It does mean a confident voice that comes from "the gut" and is grounded in the body.

⊃ Ask two girls to demonstrate, then solicit feedback from the group. Prompts, if needed: Would you take the target seriously? What could she do to make her comeback even stronger?

⊃ Each pair repeats the same scenario several times to give everyone the chance to try on both roles. Remind girls to notice how they feel in their *bodies.* While it is important to speak assertively, it is equally important to *feel* an embodied sense of confidence.

⊃ Set the stage for the second scene.

" Imagine that someone says something to you, about you, that isn't true. You know it's a lie, but they are confident and their voice is intimidating. You're being challenged to stay *self*-possessed, strong, and solid inside yourself. Let's practice 'talking back' to this person and speaking up on our own behalf."

⊃ Hand out a copy of "Comeback 2: Eyes" (H-4A) to each pair and explain the directions:

1. Choose one partner to be the harasser, one to be the target. (Roles switch later.)
2. The harasser walks up to the target, looks her straight in the eyes, and says in a mean voice, "Your eyes are blue/brown [whichever is untrue]."
3. The target responds with the first "comeback" with assertive language and body language.

⊃ Ask two girls for a volunteer demonstration and solicit feedback from the group. Prompts, if needed: Would you take the target seriously? What could she do to make her comeback even stronger? Write the following pointers on the board, review, and then ask volunteers for a repeat performance.

- Make eye contact: This signals you're not scared.
- Enunciate: Don't mumble.
- Talk in a firm tone of voice: Say it like you mean it.
- Be strong in your body.
- Negate false statements and state the truth.

⊃ Each pair repeats the scenario several times, practicing both comebacks.

⊃ At a certain point, challenge all targets to respond in *quiet* voices: "You don't have to be loud to be self-possessed."

⊃ Explain the last scene:

" In this next scene, the harasser voices an *opinion*, rather than a statement of fact (which is either true or false). She's entitled to her opinion, but so are you! Begin by acknowledging her right to an opinion—and then respectfully assert your own. Remain self-possessed. Don't allow another person's opinion to upset you or change how you think of yourself."

⊃ Hand out "Comeback 3: Shirt" (H-4A) and ask for a pair to demonstrate. The target can choose any of the four suggested comebacks. Solicit helpful group feedback.

⊃ After everyone has tried on both roles (target and harasser) give partners a chance to debrief:

1. How did it feel being the harasser?
2. How did it feel being the target?
3. How did it feel when the target "came back" at you? Did she get more powerful with practice?

☞ *Teaching Note:* If any girls say they want to hurt the harasser in return, pose a few questions in re-sponse: Does that *really* make you feel better? Think this through: What does an "eye for an eye" lead to in the long run?

🕐 *Time Check:* If you're running short on time, skip "The Cafeteria" (H-4B) and proceed to the two role plays: "The Party" (H-4C) and "The Wall" (H-4D).

The Cafeteria: Bullies and Bystanders
(Time Estimate: 10 minutes)

⊃ Ask for a volunteer to read "The Cafeteria" (H-4B) to the group.

⊃ Point out that the characters in this scene each play distinct roles. On the board, write down and review the three primary roles a person can adopt in a bullying incident:

1. *A bully or instigator.* Each of us can dish out weightism toward others. We can think, say, or do mean and unfair things based on someone's body size or shape.
2. *A target.* Each of us can be the recipient of someone else's weightist comments or actions. Someone can say, think, or do unfair things to us because of the shape or size of our bodies.
3. *A bystander.* We can witness or overhear something unfair or mean being said or done to someone else because of his or her body size or shape.

⊃ Ask the girls to describe the role played by each character in "The Cafeteria."

- Who's the instigator? (Sam sets the conflict in motion.)
- Who's the target? (Angela is the target of Sam's mean comment.)
- Who's the bystander? (Hayley witnesses the incident but doesn't say or do anything to intervene.)

⊃ Add two new definitions to the list:

1. *A follower.* Peter begins as a bystander. He becomes a follower by colluding in Sam's harassment. A follower is someone who

"falls in line" behind someone else and doesn't necessarily think for him- or herself.

2. *An activist.* No one, at this point in the scene, has assumed the courageous role of activist—someone who intervenes to stop the bullying by speaking up or taking action.

⊃ Ask each girl to put herself in Hayley's shoes: If you were a bystander who overheard this interaction, what could you do? What are your options (helpful and unhelpful)? What might an activist do in this situation? Write the girls' suggestions under the "Activist" heading.

The Party: A Role Play
(Time Estimate: 10 minutes)

⊃ Ask for three actors and one narrator for "The Party" role play. Distribute copies of the script (H-4C); then assign each girl a part and give her the corresponding nametag. Allow actors and narrator 2 minutes to rehearse (in the hall/another room).

⊃ Give all remaining girls bystander scripts (H-4D). Assign as many instigators and followers as activists to make for an exciting and realistic scenario. Explain that they will each join in and speak in the *voice of their assigned character* after the actors have concluded the rehearsed role play.

⊃ Call actors back into the room and direct them to sit scattered among the group, not set apart. Try to re-create the sense of a bunch of girls sitting around a lunch table.

⊃ Actors present the scene. At the end, invite the bystanders to join in: "You are all sitting at the same lunch table. What do *you* have to say?" Girls start by speaking from their script. Then invite everyone to improvise, remaining true to their original positions until/unless convinced to change their minds.

⊃ Debriefing Questions:

1. How did everyone feel in their roles? Was it easier to be a follower or an activist?
2. What if Jennifer were at the table? How might that affect the scene?

3. Imagine yourself in a situation like this. What would make it hard to speak up? What would it take to be an activist when all of your friends *aren't*?
4. Imagine this: You are Jennifer and you walk in and hear this. How do you feel?
5. At different points in our lives, we all can be targeted and teased like Jennifer. What do *you* usually do when someone's mean to you? Is there anything you wish you could do differently?

⊃ Concluding point:

" When we witness a weightist incident, the voices of the bully, the follower, and the activist might *all* run through our heads. The natural tendency for most of us is to be a follower, to go along with the crowd so that we don't stand out. It takes real courage, conviction, and *practice* to be a leader and an activist. The support of friends helps, too—joining together to stand our ground, like we do in this group."

The Wall: A Role Play
(Time Estimate: 5–10 minutes)

☞ *Teaching Note:* Try not to skip this! Girls love "The Wall" (H-4E) and it can be completed in 5 minutes.

⊃ Introduction:

" Imagine a situation where several people confront you with 'bad body talk.' These people are really rude, mean, and weightist—they make assumptions about you based solely on how you look. This situation would make anyone feel shaky inside. In this case, it helps if a friend steps in and 'comes back' on your behalf. Your friend can lend you his or her confidence and strength. Let's try another role play."

⊃ Before handing out the scenes, explain the guidelines:

1. Actors and narrator have 2 minutes to rehearse (in the hallway/another room).
2. Audience members play the role of activists, girls who are confident leaders. You are all

self-possessed and have the guts to stand up for each other and what you believe in.

3. Actors perform their role play. At the end, the narrator commands "FREEZE," and all actors freeze in place. At that point, one audience member can jump in and join the scene. She can join as a brand-new character, or she can tap one of the original actors on the shoulder and take her place. The narrator says "UNFREEZE" and the scene continues—with actors improvising in their roles.

4. Other audience members can command "FREEZE" at any point and step into the scene as a new character or in the place of an old character.

⊃ Ask for four actors and a narrator. Give each volunteer a nametag and a copy of the scene (H-4E) and send them into the hallway or another room to rehearse.

⊃ Ask the remaining girls to review the assertiveness skills they learned in the earlier "Comeback Kid" scenes: eye contact, a clear and firm tone of voice, and so on. Encourage them to put these skills to use in this scene.

⊃ Actors perform. Up to five audience members join in, one at a time, and improvise.

⊃ Debriefing questions:

1. Was the intervention a success? Why or why not?
2. What worked best in getting the harassers to stop?
3. Did any words or actions *escalate* the situation?
4. What else could you do or say to help your friend *without* making the situation worse? Point out the power in simple, direct language: "Stop it, that's cruel!" "C'mon, Lauren, let's go." "I can't believe you just said that!" "That's really mean." "You're really mean."

If girls come up with new and better intervention strategies, give them the chance to run through the scene again.

One-Minute Body Scan
(Time Estimate: 1 minute)

⊃ Ask everyone to sit down, close their eyes, and take a few deep breaths. Point out that simply *talking* about conflict can influence how we feel in and about our bodies.

" Slowly scan through your body, starting at the top of your head and moving your attention down through your chest, your arms, your torso, your legs, down through your feet and the tips of your toes. How does your body feel right now after so much activity and assertion?"

⊃ Prompts, if necessary: Do you feel any tension? Where do you hold tension in your body? Can you locate your center? Is it strong? Is it shaky? Are you breathing peacefully? Uncomfortably?

Call to Action Assignment
(Time Estimate: 4 minutes)

⊃ Reinforce the importance of action:

" We've covered a lot of powerful ground today here in the group. Now let's take it out into the world."

⊃ Hand each girl a "Call to Action" sheet (H-4F) and review the assignments. Answer any questions and hold girls accountable.

Closing Circle
(Time Estimate: 15 seconds)

⊃ Stand in a circle and join hands. Note the slight change in this week's declaration: "Together we make a difference, differences included."

Required "Homework"

⊃ Ask each girl to bring a popular fashion magazine to the next session. The magazines can be aimed at either girls or women (e.g., *Seventeen*, *Essence*, *Glamour*, etc.). If girls can't afford to buy magazines, check to see if your site can underwrite the cost of four or five magazines that girls can analyze in pairs.

SUPPLEMENTAL ACTIVITIES

Guest Leader

⊃ Invite an instructor in self-defense, model mugging, boxing, or kick-boxing to give a beginner's lesson to the group.

Yoga Primer 2: Standing Ground

(Time Estimate: 15 minutes)

⊃ Invite girls to try some simple yoga postures as a way to connect to an inner source of power and strength.

⊃ Turn to the "Yoga Primer" (Addendum A) and advance through the second sequence of discussion and postures:

Warm-Up Questions
Energetic Warm-Up: Wood Chopper
Mountain Pose
Warrior 2
Deep Relaxation

Getting to Know You: Interviews

(Time Estimate: 15 minutes)

⊃ In preparation, write down the following interview questions on a sheet of newsprint. Keep questions out of view until required during the activity.

1. What has changed the most in your life over the past year?
2. Who are you closest to in your family and why?
3. If you could show me your favorite place, where would you take me and what is it like?
4. Have you ever lost someone or something that was very important to you? Tell me about that.

⊃ Introduce the activity:

" Just like racism, homophobia, and other kinds of prejudice, weightism flourishes when the target of intolerance is a stranger. It's easy to talk about 'them'—be they Blacks, Whites, Hispanics, Jews, Catholics, fat people, skinny people, tall people, or short people—and say hurtful things because we don't really *know* 'them.' It's crucial to break down the 'us'/'them' barriers as we fight prejudice of any kind.

Say you see a girl and you are really tempted to judge her by the way she looks. If you really want to get to know and appreciate her, one thing you can do is ask her some open-ended questions to help you learn who she is from the 'inside out.' What do you know about open-ended questions?"

⊃ Discuss the difference between open- and closed-ended questions:

- *Closed-ended questions* are true/false or multiple-choice questions. They request only a one- or two-word reply. For example, "Do you like chocolate ice-cream?"
- *Open-ended questions* are similar to essay questions. They ask for explanations. For example, "What do you think of beauty pageants?"

⊃ Read through these examples, and ask the girls to identify whether they are closed- or open-ended questions (answers appear in parentheses):

- Where are you from? (closed)
- What's it like where you grew up? (open)
- What school do you go to? (closed)
- Is middle school different from elementary school? (closed)
- How is middle school different from elementary school? (open)
- Do you and your brother get along? (closed)
- What's your relationship like with your brother? (open)

⊃ Display the list of interview questions. Instruct girls, in pairs, to interview one another, choosing *two* questions they like best from the list. Before the girls begin, review the following "active listening" skills. During the interview, the interviewer should try to do the following:

- Make eye contact with the interviewee.
- Listen carefully without interrupting.

- Refrain from making comments or judgments.
- Say "Tell me more" or "How come?" if you don't understand something.
- End each question by asking, "Do you want to say anything else?"

⮑ *Optional:* If girls tend to be chatty, you might want to model the interview process with your co-leader. Sit facing each other, assign one person to be the interviewer, choose one of the interview questions, and be sure to actively listen without interrupting with stories of your own!

⮑ Allow 5 minutes for each interview (10 minutes in total for the two interviews). Alert the girls to switch roles when 5 minutes have passed.

⮑ Bring the girls back together as a group. Ask each girl to introduce her partner and relate one interesting thing from the interview. For example, "There's something special about [Jane] you might not know . . ."

⮑ *Optional Extension:* Girls choose one interview question and interview someone at home during the week.

Original Role Plays
(Time Estimate: 25 minutes)

⮑ Divide girls into two or three groups. Each group will write an original one-page role play. Present a general theme to be tackled in the role plays; for example, mean body comments, passive bystanders, and so on. Then assign (or solicit from the girls) a common title. Examples:

- A Sister Saves the Day
- The True Meaning of Friendship
- A Brother's Dilemma
- Too Thin to Win?
- Sibling Rivals
- I Can't Believe She Said That!
- Some Friend!

⮑ Each role play should present a dilemma requiring intervention from bystanders.

⮑ Each group performs its own role play or trades with another group.

Comic Strips
(Time Estimate: 15 minutes)

⮑ Girls work in groups of two or three. Give each group one sheet of legal-sized paper, a ruler, and black pens.

⮑ Explain the directions:

1. Draw a long rectangle on your paper and divide it into three "panels." You are going to create a cartoon script in the panels. Leave space on top to title the cartoon.
2. In panel 1, draw a cartoon of a "weightist" incident between two or three characters. Characters can be male or female, your age, younger, or older. Your cartoons can be sophisticated or simple. Stick figures are fine.
3. In panel 2, "escalate" the incident: Make it get worse.
4. Title your comic strip.
5. Leave panel 3 empty for now.

⮑ Groups swap papers. Final assignment: In panel 3, draw a viable solution to the situation depicted in panels 1 and 2.

⮑ The girls read their cartoons aloud or present them as role plays.

Unit Five:
Countering the Media Culture

ACTIVITIES

Core Activities

Action Check-In
10 Beautiful Things: A Freewrite
Personal Values
Media Values
Magazines: What's Up?
"Hi, Body" Affirmation
Call to Action Assignment
Closing Circle

Supplemental Activities

Likes and Dislikes: A Freewrite
Face-Off: A Group Collage
Editors-in-Chief
Body Portraits
Picture This: The Many Sides of Me
Thumbs Up/Thumbs Down
Video Presentation
"Boy" Magazines

OBJECTIVES

- To clarify one's own values
- To reclaim "beauty" from the media and define it for oneself
- To identify and challenge unhealthy and unrealistic media images and messages

MATERIALS AND PREPARATION

☐ Provide healthy snacks and beverages.

☐ If girls are financially able, have each one purchase one popular magazine aimed at a female audience (e.g., *Seventeen*, *Essence*, *YM*, etc.). Alternately, check magazines out of a library or see if your site can underwrite the cost of four or five magazines for girls to analyze in pairs.

☐ Photocopy one "Values Squares" handout (H-5A) per girl and enough additional copies for *pairs* of girls.

☐ Photocopy "Magazines: What's Up?" (H-5B) and cut out the squares. Each *pair* of girls gets one square.

☐ Photocopy the "'Hi, Body' Affirmation" (H-5C) and cut out one square per girl.

☐ Photocopy one "Call to Action" (H-5D) per girl.

CORE ACTIVITIES

Ground-Rule Review

↻ This is a good point in the program to remove the list of ground rules from the wall and ask the girls to recall them from memory. Ideally, the girls will internalize and carry these beyond session walls.

Healthy Comment

↻ Make a casual comment about the nutritional benefits of each snack. For example, "Cheese contains calcium, so you're less likely to break a bone. Tangerines keep your heart healthy, loaded with vitamin C."

Action Check-In
(Time Estimate: 5 minutes)

↻ Call on different girls to report on one of the three actions.

1. Everyone, can you all recite the group pledge in unison? . . . [Brittany], tell us about a time this week when you put the pledge into action.
2. Tell us about your interview. Did it inspire you?
3. Tell us about a time you stood up for yourself or someone else during the week. What happened? How did you feel? Was there another time you *wish* you'd had the guts to say something?

☞ *Teaching Note:* If anyone didn't take action, explore the reasons why. "Remember: These actions are for you. Sometimes we get overwhelmed with work, sometimes we're lazy, sometimes we're scared. What was up with you?" Affirm that it's natural to feel resistant when you're trying something new. By taking action, you invest in yourself and in your own confidence, power, and leadership: "Give yourself a chance this next week. I'll check in to see if you feel any differently after taking the action steps."

> " I was moved by the girls' lists. I realize that I am sometimes guilty of 'teenageism' and forget how deep girls are on the inside."
> —Adult leader, Laconia, New Hampshire

10 Beautiful Things: A Freewrite
(Time Estimate: 5 minutes)

↻ Ask the girls to take out their journals for a freewrite.

" Remember: This writing is for you alone. It won't be handed in or graded, and no one has to share their writing unless they want to."

↻ Write the following prompt on the board: "List 10 things you find really beautiful." Add: "These can be people, places, sounds . . . whatever's beautiful to you."

↻ Allow 3 minutes for personal writing. Leaders should participate in this activity, too.

↻ Ask for volunteers to read their lists (or portions thereof). Note how few/many girls listed physical attributes. If they listed any particular people, were they chosen because of their body shape?

🕐 *Time Check:* This is a good point to do the supplemental "Likes and Dislikes" freewriting activity. If time is short, proceed to "Personal Values."

Personal Values
(Time Estimate: 10 minutes)

↻ Hand one page of "Values Squares" (H-5A) and a pair of scissors to each girl.

↻ Ask each girl to read over the page and check "the 10 things that you value most about yourself and in your life." Encourage the girls to be honest with themselves: "Choose squares that you *really* value, not ones you think you *should* value." Girls can add values of their own on the back of extra squares.

❋ **Quiet Girls** ❋
Keep an eye out for quiet girls. Invite them to join the conversation and share what they're thinking.

➲ The girls cut out the 10 squares.

➲ Ask the girls to arrange the squares in ascending order of importance, with the most important item on the bottom. Ties are okay.

➲ Ask the girls to tape or glue their lists to a journal page or onto a piece of colored paper.

➲ Ask the girls to walk around, observe everyone's lists, and take note of which values appear most often.

➲ Discussion questions:

1. Do certain squares appear near the bottom of all the lists?
2. Which squares made your "final 10"? Which didn't and why not?
3. Can anyone guess why I asked you to put your top value on the bottom of the list? (See closing comment below.)
4. In what ways have your values changed since you were in elementary school?
5. On a scale of 1–10, how often have your *actions* reflected your values during the past week?
6. What can make it hard to live according to our own values?

➲ Closing comment:

❝ The things you value most should form the foundation for everything you do. Note that everyone has a different set of personal values. These can change throughout our lives."

❝ The discussion was intense, and I had the feeling that some of the girls were clarifying their personal values for the first time."

—Adult leader, Deerfield, New Hampshire

Media Values
(Time Estimate: 10 minutes)

The girls work in pairs of "investigation teams":

❝ Each of you is an investigative team. Imagine that you've just landed on planet Earth from outer space and you are intensely curious about the habits of human beings—particularly the lives, values, and social habits of *females*. You wander into a drugstore and see row upon row of fashion magazines lined up near the cash registers. You eagerly buy several of these magazines, figuring they'll surely give you the answers you seek."

➲ Pairs choose one magazine to investigate together: "Don't open them yet. You'll begin by investigating the *cover*."

➲ Give a new sheet of "Values Squares" (H-5A) to each pair of girls. Ask girls to scrutinize just the magazine *cover* and to check the squares that correspond to what their magazine cover indicates is most important. They can choose fewer or more than 10 squares.

❝ What does your magazine cover indicate is *most* important to its female readership? What are your eyes drawn to first? Pay attention to the written words and how they are positioned on the page, and also to the photos, body language, and facial expressions. These send messages, too."

➲ Ask girls to star one value they think the magazine presents as *most* important.

➲ Ask for several pairs to read their checked values and hold up their magazine cover for viewing.

☞ *Teaching Note:* Help the girls avoid black-and-white thinking. We don't want to insinuate that fashion magazines are all bad or to denigrate fashion models. In fact, most magazines geared toward girls and women run informative, useful articles about health, relationships, and so on. But these messages are often mixed and diluted, especially by advertising copy and images.

⊃ Discussion questions:

1. Does your magazine reflect your own personal values? Which values does it overlook?
2. Remember what you found "beautiful" in the opening freewrite. What is your magazine's idea of beauty?
3. Does your magazine present one "ideal" body type or several? If you were asked to name these body types, what names would you give them? (Examples from past groups: Skin and Bones, Victoria's Secret Babes.)
4. Is there anything *wrong* with being pretty or wanting to be pretty?

⊃ Sample wrap-up:

" There's nothing wrong with wanting to look your best. And there's nothing wrong with looking like a supermodel—*if* that's your natural, healthy body shape. The problem is that 95% of us aren't genetically wired to look like models—without doing some really unhealthy and damaging things to our bodies. If you're 5'3", you're never going to be 5'10". Bodies come in all shapes and sizes! There's nothing wrong with being short, muscular, stocky, or big-boned. There is something wrong, however, with not caring for the miraculous body you've inherited.

When we're surrounded by so many 'perfect' images of 'pretty,' we can start to think there's something wrong with us if we don't look like a model. It can be challenging to accept the body you have. But it's really empowering! Self-acceptance keeps you from wasting precious time and energy thinking you'll be a happier person if you could only make yourself over into someone you're not.

When it comes to beauty, we need to develop wider eyes: to see 'pretty' and 'beauty' in more than one narrow way. So go ahead and read one of these magazines, if you like, but remember who you are! It's not that looks don't matter, but keep in mind *what matters most to you*! Remember those things that you found beautiful. Hold to those aspects of your lives that you value most."

Magazines: What's Up?
(Time Estimate: 15 minutes)

⊃ Girls continue in pairs. Give each pair a different assignment square from "Magazines: What's Up?" (H-5B). Answer any questions and allow the girls 5 minutes to complete their assignments.

⊃ Check in with each pair to keep girls on track. Remind girls to pay attention to both copy and photos.

⊃ Pairs report on their investigations.

☞ *Teaching Note:* Girls tend to make sweeping generalizations during this discussion. While it's okay to allow the girls space to vent their feelings about magazines, commercial culture, and professional models, help to focus their attention on *specific* pages, ads, copy, and photographs. For example, Can you show us a specific *image* of that idea in your magazine? What *exactly* is it about that photo that makes it so compelling, that makes you react so strongly? Read us some specific *words* that send that message.

☞ *Teaching Note:* Be prepared to devote extra time to debriefing the "three photographs that are about sexiness and getting attention from boys or men." This discussion may feel like opening a can of worms, but it is *crucial* to name and discuss how females get objectified in both fashion magazines and mainstream society.

⊃ Discussion questions:

1. Agree or disagree: Models look the same in person as they do on the cover of a magazine.
2. Studies show that after just 15 minutes of reading fashion magazines, girls and women feel crummy and worse about themselves. Can anyone guess why? Comment: Advertisers want us to believe that we have to buy something and change ourselves to be happy and valued. Advertisers want your money, and they'll do anything to get it—including making you feel insecure.

3. Many fashion magazines present girls and women as "sex objects." Can anyone explain or guess what that term means?

4. Agree or disagree: You need to pose and dress like a sex object in order to be sexy and get asked out.

5. Here's a statement made by a girl who was in another Full of Ourselves group: "Guys mainly like girls for their breast size and looks." What do you think? Call to mind several boys you know: What do they think?

6. Do people look at you in a different way now that you're no longer a little kid? Has anyone ever "checked you out"? How did you feel?

7. On TV and in advertisements, what do guys seem to value most in girls? Do you think this is true about people who really love each other?

⥀ Sample wrap-up:

❝ Sometimes the media present female bodies as objects on display—to be scanned and rated and touched without permission. Popular music sometimes gives the message that what matters most about a young woman is her body *parts* and how well these add up. This process is called *objectification*: the reducing of a fascinating, multidimensional person—with talents, needs, dreams, thoughts, and feelings, as well as a body, to a one-dimensional *object*. There's a big difference between being an object and being a person in all your complexity.

Of course, none of you is merely a body. You're not human *objects*; you are human *beings* who are capable of loving and being sexual when the time is safe and right according to your values."

🕐 *Time Check:* This a good point at which to do the supplemental "Face-Off" collage. If time is running short, proceed to the "'Hi, Body' Affirmation."

"Hi, Body" Affirmation
(Time Estimate: 5 minutes)

⥀ *Teaching Note:* After focusing on surface appearances and media-manufactured images, it's important to give girls the chance to connect with themselves.

⥀ Ask the girls to find a comfortable spot on the floor and lie down for a guided meditation. Explain that the meditation was created by girls their age who went through this same program. It might be a little hokey, but it's an example of how we can befriend our bodies. Ask girls to listen and follow along in their imaginations. Read the following script in a calm voice, pausing for 5 seconds or more between sentences.

❝ Close your eyes and take a few deep breaths to connect with your body . . . [5-second pause] . . . Feel the floor supporting your weight . . . Notice any sounds in the room, and bring your attention back to your breathing . . . Let any thoughts or worries flow away on your breath like waves.

You are just waking up in the morning . . . Imagine yourself getting up and looking in a full-length mirror as you think about what you are going to wear . . . Here's what you say to yourself: 'Hi, Body. You are going to carry me through this day. Because of you, I can dance, I can see, I can taste, I can sing, I can kiss . . . With your help, I can show the world who I am today . . . I will take really good care of you because you are my only body . . . And as I love and respect you, you'll take good care of me . . . We are allies; you stand up for me and I stand up for you, no matter what anyone else says . . . We'll be friends through thick and thin. We're friends for life.' . . . You get dressed, eat breakfast, and head out into your day . . .

Now gently bring your attention back to your breathing . . . Notice any sounds and sensations in the room . . . When you feel ready, open your eyes and come back to sitting."

⥀ Discussion questions:

1. Does anyone feel differently from when we started?
2. Do any of you ever talk to yourselves in such a nice way?
3. Do any of you ever talk to yourselves in a mean way?

⥀ Sample wrap-up:

❝ Everyone has critical voices that run through their heads. No one can expect to drown these out once and for all. But we can try to pay attention to our thoughts so that our internalized 'bully' doesn't beat us up without our even realizing it."

⊃ Hand out "'Hi, Body' Affirmation" squares (H-5C) for the girls to use in this week's "Call to Action."

Call to Action Assignment

(Time Estimate: 3 minutes)

⊃ Reinforce the importance of action: "Let's take what we've learned out into the world—to change the world!"

⊃ Distribute "Call to Action" handouts (H-5D), review the assignments, and answer any questions.

Closing Circle

(Time Estimate: 15 seconds)

⊃ Stand in a circle, join hands, and affirm in unison: "Together we make a difference, differences included."

SUPPLEMENTAL ACTIVITIES

Likes and Dislikes: A Freewrite

(Time Estimate: 8 minutes)

⊃ Pose two sentence stems, in turn, allowing time for the girls to complete each thought in writing.

1. I like fashion magazines because . . .
2. I don't like fashion magazines because . . .

⊃ Go around the circle and ask the girls to share their opinions.

☞ *Teaching Note:* Try to remain impartial. If girls sense that adult leaders have a preconceived stance on fashion magazines, they will likely say what they think *you* want to hear. The goal of this unit is to encourage open discussion and to raise awareness, not to bash fashion magazines.

Face-Off: A Group Collage

(Time Estimate: 8 minutes)

⊃ This collage can be created in less than 10 minutes. You'll need scissors, glue sticks, black pens, and one sheet of oaktag. Draw a circle on the oaktag, leaving some space around the edges where the girls can write.

⊃ Hand out scissors and instruct the girls to cut or tear out female *faces* from their magazines: large faces, small faces, no bodies, no necks, just faces and hair.

⊃ Have the girls glue overlapping faces inside the circle to create a collage.

⊃ While girls are cutting and gluing, encourage conversation. Pose casual questions and comments to the group:

- Funny how they look so similar. Any of these girls having a bad-hair day?
- Anyone wearing glasses? Braces? Any pimples? Birthmarks? Moles? Bushy eyebrows? Runny noses?
- Not many girls of color, Indian girls, Asian faces, or chubby faces, huh? Who's left out?
- The beauty industry rakes in $13 billion a year. How many college educations would that buy? With that kind of money, we could fund a girls' baseball league or cure world hunger!
- If these faces could talk, what would they be saying? Draw "talk bubbles" around the margins of the collage and have the faces "talk."
- Would you like to say anything to the fashion stylists who create these images? Write in the margins. (Examples from past participants: Get real! No plastic surgery allowed! Don't have her just look pretty, have her do something! Eat!)

⊃ Give girls black pens and challenge them to alter the faces so that they look more realistic. For example, add pimples, facial hair, glasses, and so on.

⊃ Display the "defaced" collage in a prominent place.

Editors-in-Chief
(Time Estimate: 30 minutes or an entire session)

⊃ Divide girls into two groups and explain the assignment:

" Your assignment: A major publisher has hired you as editors-in-chief of a brand-new magazine aimed at girls your age. You've been given the go-ahead to design whatever you want. Discuss and decide what you'd like to create, starting with the title, subject matter, layout ideas, departments, and so on. The sky's the limit; anything's possible. Your magazine can cover poetry, water-skiing, physics, fashion, finger painting, or any combination of topics you want. Together, design your dream publication.

Your publisher has requested that you submit a detailed magazine summary and description by this deadline: _____."

⊃ If the girls are ambitious, challenge them to create a sample issue incorporating original artwork, writing, computer layout and graphics, and so on.

Body Portraits
(Time Estimate: 30+ minutes)

⊃ This interactive art activity is a powerful way for girls to get in touch with their bodies and themselves.

⊃ *Preparation:* Bring in large sheets of paper to be used for tracing body outlines, along with thick black markers. You can find reams of brown wrapping/mural paper at many art shops. Also supply a variety of materials for use in the collage: paints and paintbrushes, crayons, magazines, fabric, beads, feathers, scissors, glue, and so on.

⊃ The girls work in pairs. Each pair gets two big sheets of mural paper. Each girl traces the outline of her partner's body. Girls can lie on the paper in any position: flat on their backs, spread-eagled, one leg crooked, and so on.

⊃ Ask girls to decorate their body outlines using the materials on hand. You can leave directions open-ended or suggest options. For example, "Fill your body in with your dreams, your interests, the colors of your personality, and affirmations."

⊃ If girls like the idea, display body portraits around the room.

Picture This: The Many Sides of Me
(Time Estimate: Over the course of 1 week)

⊃ Supply each girl with a 12-exposure disposable camera.

⊃ The girls work in pairs. The assignment: "Take 12 pictures that depict the many sides of you. Ask your partner to shoot the pictures that involve you."

⊃ Collect the cameras and have the film developed. Girls create and present personal photo essays.

Thumbs Up/Thumbs Down
(Time Estimate: Homework, plus 10 minutes during group)

⊃ Ask girls or pairs of girls to bring a discerning eye to MTV and videotape *two* music videos to bring to the group. One video should present positive images/lyrics about females, the other negative images/lyrics.

⊃ View and analyze the music videos as a group.

Video Presentation
(Time Estimate: 20 minutes)

⊃ Obtain either of these suggested videos: "Beyond Killing Us Softly" or "Slim Hopes." Call your local public library, a nearby university library, a women's center, or the central office of your school district to see if they have copies of either video that you can borrow.

⊃ Secure a TV and VCR/DVD player.

⊃ View the video before showing it to the group. Will the entire video hold the girls' attention? Would it be better to show a short portion?

➲ Ask the girls to write up a "movie review" for their school paper.

"Boy" Magazines

(Time Estimate: 15 minutes)

➲ Bring in several magazines that are marketed directly to boys and/or men. Repeat the "Media Values" assignment. Contrast these magazines to those marketed to girls and women.

Unit Six:
Nourishing Our Bodies

ACTIVITIES

Core Activities

    Action Check-In

    Eating: A Questionnaire and Debriefing

    Power Foods/Junk Foods

    Conscious Eating: A Sensational Experience

    Mommy, May I?

    Call to Action Assignment

    Closing Circle

Supplemental Activities

    Freewrite: "I Am Hungry"

    Picnic in the Park

    Athletic Game or Outdoor Activity

OBJECTIVES

- To equip girls to make more nutritious choices on their own behalf
- To encourage variety and flexibility in a daily diet
- To promote the importance of eating three meals a day
- To promote healthy snacking in response to hunger signals
- To replace the rigid notion of "good" versus "bad" foods with the idea of more or less "powerful" foods
- To understand the difference between "dieting" and having a healthy diet
- To dispel myths about dietary fat
- To experience the pleasures of "conscious eating"
- To promote greater body acceptance

MATERIALS AND PREPARATION

- ☐ Supply raisins, chocolate kisses, and small paper cups for the "Conscious Eating" activity.
- ☐ Supply other healthy snacks and drinks to *follow* the "Conscious Eating" activity.
- ☐ Review the "Troubleshooting" section at the end of this unit.
- ☐ For "Eating: A Questionnaire and Debriefing," photocopy one questionnaire (H-6A) per girl and review the "Answer Guide" found at the end of this unit.
- ☐ For the "Power Foods/Junk Foods" discussion, photocopy "Snack Attack!" (H-6B). Draw up a sheet of newsprint with two headings— "Power Foods" and "Junk Foods"—and their distinguishing features before the start of the session.
- ☐ Photocopy one "What Is Normal Eating?" (H-6C) per girl.
- ☐ For "Mommy, May I?," cut the scenarios on the "Mommy, May I?" handout (H-6D) into six strips and place them in a paper bag. Review the "Answer Guide" for "Mommy, May I?" found at the end of this unit.
- ☐ Photocopy one "Call To Action" (H-6E) per girl.

CORE ACTIVITIES

Ground-Rule Review

⊃ Ask girls to review ground rules from memory.

Healthy Comment

⊃ Make a casual comment about the nutritional benefits of each snack. For example, "Peanuts and raisins both help you think better; they're loaded with vitamin B_1, also called thiamine. The B vitamins in cheddar cheese support your memory and help calm your nerves when you get stressed out."

Action Check-In

(Time Estimate: 5–10 minutes)

⊃ Girls report on action steps from the last unit. Reserve most of the time to review the letters of protest.

1. Tell us about appreciating your body this week. Was that challenging to do?
2. What did you do with your list of beautiful things? How did you bring more beauty into your life this week?
3. Did you decide to boycott any magazines? Did you get your parents to come on board with you?
4. I'd like to hear the letters of protest. Who'd like to volunteer to read theirs first?

Eating: A Questionnaire and Debriefing

(Time Estimate: 15 minutes)

⊃ Girls work in pairs. Hand out one copy of "Eating: A Questionnaire" (H-6A) to each pair and allow the girls 2 minutes to complete it together. If the girls disagree with a statement or are undecided, ask them to write down the reason why or what further information they need to come to a conclusive decision.

⊃ Debrief the girls after they take the quiz. Review statements in turn, asking for a show of hands: "How many of you agreed with this statement?" Ask *one* pair to explain their reasoning (whether correct or not). As needed, supplement girls' answers with information from the "Answer Guide."

⊃ A few points to keep in mind while debriefing specific statements:

- Statement 3: Draw a clear distinction between *going on* a fad weight-loss "diet" and a person's daily "diet."
- Statement 9: Ask girls to come up with their own definitions of "normal" eating, and then distribute "What Is Normal Eating?" (H-6C). Go around the room asking each girl to read a separate point.
- Springboard straight from statement 10 into the following discussion of what constitutes a "power" food.

☞ *Teaching Note:* The "Answer Guide" is offered as *background* information for adult leaders. It's best not to read answers aloud in their entirety. Instead, highlight key points before the session to draw on as needed during the debriefing. It's best to keep the pace moving so that the discussion doesn't get bogged down and feel too much like Health class. When possible, present information in the form of questions that ask girls to draw on their own experience. For example, "Have you ever noticed that it's easier to concentrate in morning classes if you've eaten breakfast?"

❀ Teaching Note ❀

It's crucial to make no judgments about how or what girls eat. For some girls, chips might provide the highest source of energy during the day, or eating snacks may be the only safe way they know to deal with anxiety. Investigate resources and people in your community to whom you can point girls who need extra support. If you have questions, seek out the nutritionist at your doctor's office, through your health plan, or at a local community health clinic.

Power Foods/Junk Foods
(Time Estimate: 10 minutes)

⟴ Ask the girls to give you three examples of "junk foods" followed by three examples of "power-packed" (i.e., nutritious) foods. Record the girls' answers on the board under two columns titled "Power Foods" and "Junk Foods."

⟴ Ask the girls, "What makes these types of foods different from one another?" Ask them to come up with broader definitions of the two food categories.

⟴ Supplement the girls' answers with the prepared newsprint. Review the lists, being sure to point out that foods fall along a *continuum* (as shown in the table that follows). Foods can be *more* or *less* powerful depending on their form and how they are prepared.

Main Features	"Power-Packed" Foods	Junk Foods
What's in it?	Packed with nutrients Low in added fat, salt, or sugar	Packed with additives Often fatty, salty, sugary
What form is it in?	Unprocessed; whole, natural, organic	Processed with chemicals, dyes, preservatives
How is it presented?	Often unpackaged	Often packaged
How is it prepared?	Steamed, broiled, grilled; not much grease	Often fried and greasy

⟴ Offer the following statement: "Depending on its form and how it's prepared, the *same food* can be *more or less* powerful. Let's see if you can tell the difference." Record girls' answers to the following questions under the appropriate heading on the chart (sample answers appear in parentheses).

1. When is an apple most powerful? (in natural form, apple juice)
2. When is an apple junky? (candy apple, processed fruit roll-up)
3. When is it somewhere in the middle?" (homemade apple pie)

⟴ Repeat with *popcorn, potato, fish.* Allow girls 1 minute to come up with three examples for each food along a continuum: most powerful, less powerful, least powerful (junk). Record answers on newsprint. Your chart should look similar to the following example.

Type of Food	Most Powerful → → →		Least Powerful
popcorn	air-popped	light butter	movie popcorn, caramel corn
potato	baked potato	chips	french fries, hash browns
fish	broiled	grilled fish	fried fish sticks

⟴ Pose the following questions and compile a list of answers to item 3:

1. How many of you snack?
2. Agree or disagree: Snacking is good for you.
3. What are your all-time favorite snacks?

⟴ Hand out and review "Snack Attack!" (H-6B).

⟴ *Optional:* Include a copy of the "Snack Attack!" handout with the next letter you send home to parents.

⟴ Sample wrap-up:

❝ When we eat foods in their most powerful form, they give us the most power. On the other hand, if *most* of what we eat is junk, after a while our bodies will wind up feeling tired or wired and junky. This isn't to say that we shouldn't ever eat junk foods. Most people do now and then. That's part of normal eating! The important thing is to try to eat a *variety* of foods every day—and to keep the balance tipped in favor of power foods."

Conscious Eating:
A Sensational Experience
(Time Estimate: 5 minutes)

⟴ Hand out a small cup of raisins to each girl and invite everyone to eat a few. (Confirm that no one is allergic to raisins.) Explain the activity:

❝ It's important to be conscious not only about *what* we eat but about *how* we eat. Eating's not only nutritional, it's sensational. We get to smell food with our noses, taste it with our taste buds, feel the texture of food in our mouths and the warmth and weight of food in our tummies. How many of you are fast eaters? Have you ever slowed down to really notice and savor every bite of the food you eat? Let's try an experiment. Everybody sit back and get comfortable. It's difficult to enjoy food if we're anxious or tense. Close your eyes, take a few deep breaths, get quiet, notice how you feel inside. Let your thoughts just drift through your mind like clouds through the sky. Follow each breath you take, the inhale and the exhale."

⊃ Once the group has settled down, give these instructions:

- Everyone open your eyes, take *one* raisin from your cup and look at it closely . . .
- Notice its shape, its color, its wrinkles . . .
- Now smell your raisin . . .
- Now close your eyes and put the raisin on your tongue. Notice its texture and its weight . . .
- Move the raisin around in your mouth . . . It might start to get soft, maybe even start to dissolve . . .
- Notice the raisin's taste . . . Where in your mouth does it taste the sweetest? The strongest? . . .
- Now chew your raisin and take in the sensation of sweetness . . .
- Swallow your raisin and pay attention to the sensation of swallowing . . .

⊃ Ask girls to compare the difference between the first and second raisin-eating experience. Point out that when we remain conscious of what's happening *internally* when we eat, eating becomes a sensational and very fulfilling experience. Now read through the script a second time, asking girls to consciously eat a chocolate kiss or chocolate chip.

☞ *Teaching Note:* Don't begin with the sugar; it zaps the taste buds.

⊃ Sample debriefing:

" Few people eat this slowly in their daily lives. The point is to try to remain as 'awake' and aware as

possible when we eat so that the experience is as 'sense-sational' as possible. This means making an effort to eat without external distractions such as watching TV, reading, or having an emotional discussion during a meal."

⊃ Pose the question, "How would you define *normal* eating?" Compile a list of answers. Afterwards, distribute and review "What Is Normal Eating?" (H-6C).

Mommy, May I?
(Time Estimate: 15 minutes)

⊃ Divide girls into six groups. Introduce the assignment in this manner:

" Let's assume you are all moms. You each have one daughter whom you adore, an 8-year-old growing girl. Above all else, you want her to be healthy, happy, strong, and energetic. Being a mommy requires constant troubleshooting and limit-setting. Little girls don't always follow directions; sometimes they whine and beg and ask for things that aren't good for them."

⊃ Invite a girl from each group to pull out one "Mommy, May I?" strip of paper from the paper bag. Allow groups 3 minutes to decide how they'll respond, as moms, in the given scenario. Repeat: "Remember, above all else, you want your little daughter to be healthy, happy, strong, and energetic."

⊃ Ask the group of "moms" who planned a daily menu to report first. As girls report their menu, list foods on or near either the "power-packed foods" or "junk food" column on the newsprint used in the "Power Foods/Junk Foods" activity.

⊃ Ask the girls if they can list the five main food groups: grains, fruits, vegetables, meats, milk/dairy. Write these on the board. If the daily menu is missing any food groups, ask for suggestions on how the meals/snacks could be modified. Point out that missed food groups can be made up in the *next meal* or on the *next day*.

⊃ Ask the remaining groups to present their situation and response(s). As girls explain what they'd

> **"** I loved how the girls were protective of their 8-year-olds!"
>
> —Adult leader, Tulsa, Oklahoma

say to their daughters, invite them to try on the role of "mommy" and role-play dialogue. As needed, offer insights from the "Answer Guide" for "Mommy, May I?"

Call to Action Assignment
(Time Estimate: 5 minutes)

⊃ Hand out the "Call to Action" (H-6E) and review the assignments.

⊃ Answer questions and hold the girls accountable for reporting on their action steps at the start of the next session.

Closing Circle
(Time Estimate: 15 seconds)

⊃ Stand in a circle, join hands, and declare in unison: "Together we make a difference, differences included."

SUPPLEMENTAL ACTIVITIES

Freewrite: "I Am Hungry"
(Time Estimate: 5–10 minutes)

⊃ Introduction:

" Freewrites are a way for us to get in touch with ourselves, with what we really think and feel. This writing is for you alone and can take any form: a journal entry, story, poem, letter, dialogue between fictitious characters. You might opt to draw a picture."

⊃ Ask the girls to take a few deep breaths and collect their thoughts. Write the following prompt on the board or a sheet of newsprint: "I am hungry for . . ."

⊃ Allow the girls several minutes for writing. Adult leaders should participate in this activity, too.

⊃ Ask for volunteers to read freewrites aloud.

Picnic in the Park
(Time Estimate: One Session)

⊃ Plan an outdoor picnic, weather permitting, or an indoor picnic on a blanket spread out on the floor. Each group member contributes a favorite food item to the menu, making sure all five food groups—plus a little something sweet and fattening—are represented. Encourage the girls to bring homemade foods and to cook with one another. Combine the picnic with the following outdoor sport/activity.

Athletic Game or Outdoor Activity
(Time Estimate: 45+ minutes)

⊃ Ask the girls to name sports and outdoor activities that they enjoy or that they'd like to learn more about. Then schedule an extra session and go to the gym to shoot hoops, go to the park to play ball, invite a local tai chi teacher to volunteer an hour with your group, and so forth.

A SECTION FOR ADULT LEADERS

Troubleshooting: Unit 6

The girls may pose challenging questions during this unit. Here are some typical questions, along with suggested responses.

1. How much should I eat? Should I count calories to figure that out?

A typical healthy diet consists of three meals and several healthy snacks each day. Your own appetite is an exquisite barometer of your energy and food needs. Tune into your own body—you can use your conscious eating experience—to help you determine when you are hungry and when you are full. Stop to notice *when* you're hungry and *why* you're hungry. Does your body need fuel, or are you hungry for emotional reasons?

Appetites are influenced by many different things. Does anyone know what causes your appetite to change? Stress, activity level, hydration level, and where you are in your menstrual cycle—even boredom—to name a few factors. With all these variables constantly in flux, it's really important to stay connected to your body, your feelings, and your knowledge about nutrition.

2. What's the best way for me to lose weight?

First of all, you may need to check out whether or not weight loss is something that is needed and healthy for you. Some kids, those who are already eating well and exercising regularly, don't need to lose any weight—although they might feel pressure to diet from magazines or from their friends. (Remember: Friends don't let friends starve themselves.)

Other kids, those who "veg out" a lot and eat junk food, gain unnecessary weight that would be healthy to lose. If that's you or someone you know, first cut down on the junk food. Then get up off of the couch and move! Try walking vigorously for 20 minutes a few times a week. A sound prescription for losing weight is to exercise moderately, eat a variety of healthy foods, and take better care of your body all around. If you don't know what healthy eating means for you, talk to a health professional; start with the school nurse or nutritionist or your doctor.

3. What about Weight Watchers? My Aunt Susie swears by it.

Some diet programs are better than others. The better ones help people learn how to eat balanced meals and the basics of nutrition. They teach you how to eat real food (not special drinks or "nutrition" bars) and how to develop healthy eating habits that work in real places—in school, at home, at restaurants, and so on. They also guide you to lose weight slowly—at most 1–2 pounds over 1–2 weeks—because rapid weight loss usually leads to rapid weight gain.

The worst diet programs promise miracles. They give people the message that they can lose a lot of weight quickly and keep it off forever. Sometimes they use scare tactics: They give the message that certain foods are "bad," that having an appetite is "bad," and that a person isn't "good" enough unless she changes her body. Messages like these make it hard, if not impossible, to be powerful, healthy leaders in the world.

Anything that interrupts your own personal respectful response to your hunger is not going to work in the long run. Hunger and fullness signals are a communication from your body. To ignore them is to ignore a fundamental piece of self-care and self-respect. If you don't pay attention to its signals, your body will lose confidence in your ability to take care of it.

Strict diet plans cause you to lose your natural ability to regulate food intake. Your body will stop sending you clear hunger or satisfaction signals. It becomes harder to read your body's subtle signals that tell you when you're hungry and full. What's most important is that we all stay connected to our own bodies and our own needs.

4. What about over-the-counter diet pills as a way to lose weight fast?

Diet pills can be dangerous and addictive, and they have bad side effects. They falsify your body's experience of fullness. They create an illusion in your body. Your body, in the long run, is smarter than a pill.

5. Can I use laxatives and diuretics to lose weight?

Laxatives and diuretics, like diet pills, can be extremely dangerous. If someone uses laxatives or diuretics often, their body can naturally stop processing fluids and foods and become dependent on these unnatural prompts. They can also cause unhealthy mineral loss and serious heart problems.

6. How about Slimfast and other liquid supplements?

What do you think is wrong with this picture? A packaged can meal is only as good as our recent research—and science is still in the dark about a lot of things concerning nutrition. You just can't beat real foods! Humans haven't been able to improve on what nature provides (whole grains, fruits, vegetables). Learning to eat a variety of power-packed, healthy foods according to your own internal hunger cues is the best thing you can do for your overall health and well-being. Drinking Slimfast is not the answer. It's only another promise of a quick fix.

7. If I take vitamins, I don't need to eat, right?

The best way to get vitamins is directly from food. Just taking vitamins alone isn't enough. That is why vitamins are called supplements. They are meant to "add more," but not to be the only supply of nutrients in your diet.

8. Will boys only like me if I'm thin?

That's the message the media feed boys and girls, but research has shown repeatedly that it's not true. Even though boys sometimes say mean things about girls' bodies, boys have a wider perspective of what's attractive than many girls do. In fact, boys say that they don't like being around girls who talk about diets (boring!) and that it's no fun going on a date with a girl who won't eat and enjoy food. Most relationships occur because you see someone frequently and have common interests, not because of what one person is wearing or weighing.

A SECTION FOR ADULT LEADERS

Answer Guide— Eating: A Questionnaire

These answers are not intended to be read aloud verbatim. Instead, use this background information to supplement the girls' answers.

1. Eating makes you smart.

Have you ever noticed that if you don't eat, you get tired and zone-out a lot more easily? This can be a big problem in the middle of class or a conversation. Your brain needs fuel to think, so if you skip lunch you are undercutting your education. Without essential nutrients, your body has to work much harder to pay attention both in and outside of school.

2. Everyone's healthiest adult size and shape is genetically preprogrammed at birth.

Only 3% of the population is genetically predisposed to be very tall and very thin—in spite of media messages that imply anyone can look like a model. That means 97% of us can't fit the very narrow beauty ideal without causing real harm to our health and our bodies.

Just like your natural hair type and eye color are inherited, so is the healthiest natural weight range for you as an adult. Every person is born with a genetic predisposition to be a certain healthy shape and size. These are "set" in the hypothalamus region of the brain. This "set point" is like a thermostat set to your own particular healthiest weight range. Your body will work to stay within this range because it wants you to be strong and healthy.

Some people are born to have broad shoulders, big strong bones, and a rounder middle. They won't look like a skin-and-bones model because their bodies are built to be bigger and stronger: That's what's healthiest and "most beautiful" for them. Remember: Bodies come in different shapes and sizes. The challenge for all of us is to maintain the healthiest bodies we can, through healthy exercise and healthy eating, given our genetic predispositions.

3. A lot of diets don't work, especially "fad" diets found in magazines.

Here's what most people and commercials don't tell you about diets: 98% of all diets (that aren't supervised by a doctor or nutritionist) cause you to *gain* weight, not lose it. Can anyone guess why?

Studies show that starving yourself all day can leave you so hungry that you'll eat everything in sight later, regardless of whether this is power or junk food. Also, when you diet or go without eating, your blood sugar drops. When it drops very low, your brain assumes you're starving and drives you to eat. When people get this hungry, they usually crave "quick-carbo" foods (chips, candy, ready-to-eat cereals) for fast energy and often wind up eating more than they need. If you consistently don't eat enough, your metabolism will actually slow down and your body will try to hold onto its fat.

Have you ever seen one of those ads in which a woman testifies: "I lost 120 pounds in 6 months!" These ads aren't regulated. No one checks to see if these claims are true or not. Two years later, that same woman has typically gained back all of the weight, plus some, and the "yo-yo" effect of weight loss and gain has wreaked havoc on her body. Here are some medical statistics about people who go on medically unregulated diets: After 6 months they regain 50% of the weight they may have initially lost. After 1 year, they've gained 100% of the weight back, if not more. Fad diets can't be trusted.

People who are overweight and need to lose weight for health reasons need to go on a medically supervised diet, *not* a magazine diet. They need a diet that's about changing their entire lifestyle, including how and what they eat, exercise habits, stress management, and so on. Your doctor or the school nurse can help you determine what's healthy and best for you.

The best thing you can do to stay at your body's healthiest weight is to exercise moderately and eat well: a variety of foods (not junk food!) based on your knowledge of nutrition and in response to your tummy's hunger signals, not according to rules imposed by a diet.

4. It's okay to eat yummy treats, but when you're mad or upset about something, eating will not take away the real source of the problem.

Overeating when you're mad (or bored, or lonely, or frustrated) might temporarily numb your feelings, but it can lead to unhealthy weight gain and it doesn't help you deal with the *real* problem. In other words, if you're mad at someone, tell them. A double-scoop sundae might taste good, but it won't solve the relationship problem.

When under stress many people try to "swallow" or "stuff" their emotions, rather than deal directly with what's bothering them. It's important to ask yourself, "What am I really hungry for? Am I hungry for food or am I hungry for help . . . love . . . connection . . . friendship?"

There's nothing wrong with eating "comfort foods" now and then—everybody does. But if the *only* way you respond to difficult situations is by eating, you'll probably put on unneeded weight *and* you'll miss an opportunity to stand up for yourself and have a voice.

5. Eating makes you strong.

Not only that, eating keeps us alive! Eating helps you run faster, jump higher, swim farther, and think better. It makes you more graceful and coordinated. It also gives you energy to get through the day and cope with all the stresses that are thrown your way. Does eating help your muscles and bones? Your bones grow until the age of 20, so it's particularly important that you get enough calcium and protein to help develop strong bones.

Remember: It's important to eat a balanced, healthy diet. Unhealthy eating—eating lots of junk food or binge-eating—makes you tired, numb, lethar-

gic, and overweight. If you eat too many of the wrong foods too often, you can suffer from malnutrition.

6. Vegetables are indispensable, but most important for a healthy diet is variation.

If all you ate were vegetables, your diet would not be healthy. For optimum health, you need to eat a balanced and varied diet so that your body gets all of the nutrients you need: dietary fats, proteins, carbohydrates, vitamins, minerals, and water. Our bodies have minimum thresholds for each of these essential nutrients. For example, if you don't have water for 4 or 5 days, you can die. If you don't have a minimum amount of fat, your system can shut down. Our bodies need all of these nutrients, and they all work in concert.

7. Everyone needs to eat different-sized portions of food because everyone's body has different needs.

When you're standing on line in the cafeteria, it's tempting to take more food or less food based on what someone else puts on his or her plate. But only *you* know how hungry you are, how hard you're pushing your body, how high or low your energy is, and what you've already eaten that day. There are also nutritional guides that define a "standard portion" for the average person; these provide a good starting point. But you're the only one who can make the right food choices for yourself.

Portion sizes vary depending on your appetite and what you've already eaten that day, your metabolism, where you are in your menstrual cycle, and your activity level. For instance, an athlete or dancer who works out 3 hours daily needs more food than someone who's less active. The best way to determine the right-sized portion is to tune in to your own appetite.

Have you ever noticed that right before your period you get hungrier? That's because your hormones shift, causing physiological changes in your body. Your metabolism speeds up by 10%-20%, so you might crave, and naturally need, more food than usual. Also, your endorphin level drops, which might be one reason why many of us crave chocolate around our periods. Research suggests that chocolate boosts endorphin levels. You don't have to eat a ton of it. Three or four chocolate kisses will usually do.

If you don't know what portions are right for you, talk to your doctor or to the school nurse or nutritionist. If you are an athlete or working out regularly, you need to take responsibility for finding out how much *extra* you need to eat to fuel your body. Start by talking to your coach.

8. Fat is a vital part of a healthy diet. Fat is crucial to your health and well-being.

Without dietary fat, your body can't construct the cells that make up every part of you. Fat keeps your heart healthy. Fat makes your hair lustrous and shiny and keeps your skin from becoming dry and flaky. Fat transports vitamins to right where they're needed in your body. Fat keeps you from becoming irritable and a bundle of nerves. Fat buffers each nerve cell in your body with essential fatty acids. Fat gives your muscles the energy needed to move through the day. Fat helps build strong bones. Without fat in your diet, you're more likely to break a leg and get stress fractures. And don't forget that dietary fat makes foods flavorful and yummy. Not only that, fat sends the first signal to the brain that your body has been fed and you've had enough to eat. That means that you'll feel more satisfied after eating low-fat yogurt than fat-free yogurt.

Some dietary fats are healthier than others. The "good guys" are the unsaturated fats found in vegetable oils, nuts, and seeds. Some of the "bad guys" are saturated fats found in things like packaged cookies and candy. But as long as you're eating lots of fruits and vegetables each day, your body should be able to make good use of any kind of fat.

9. It's important to eat three meals each day so that you have energy to think, move, interact with friends, cope with stresses, and pay attention in class.

Just like cars need to refuel with gasoline in order to run, we need to regularly refuel our bodies—or we'll run out of energy!

How many of you ate breakfast this morning? What did you eat for breakfast? Is that a *meal*? What is "a meal" anyway? There's no single definition, but it's important to think about eating a *variety* of foods, a balance of food groups and nutrients. What are the five main food groups? Each of the food groups provide *some*, but not all, of the nutrients you need to stay healthy and strong. That's why it's so important to eat a *variety* of foods every day: some fruits and vegetables, some grains, some proteins like eggs for breakfast or tuna for lunch, some fats, some dairy products for strong bones.

How would you define "normal eating"? (Hand out "What Is Normal Eating?" [H-6C].) What if you miss a meal one day, is this "bad"? Everyone misses a meal now and then. That's normal! But if you miss meals on a regular basis, you're probably not getting the nutrients and energy you need to feel and live your best.

10. Snacking can be very healthy for you—it depends on whether or not you're hungry and what you snack on.

If you're hungry after school, that means your body needs energy, so snacking is a great idea! But what kind of energy will you give yourself? Some foods are power packed: loaded with vitamins and minerals and protein and other nutrients. Others are "junky": They might taste good, but they don't have much nutritional value and leave you feeling hungry for more and tired soon after you eat them.

We all eat junks foods now and then; that's normal. But if *all* we eat is junk, sooner or later this will affect our energy level, our brain power, our health, and our weight. The important point is to try to be *conscious* of whether or not you're hungry and of getting enough "power" foods in your daily diet.

A SECTION FOR ADULT LEADERS

Answer Guide—Mommy, May I?

As a mommy, you're responsible for planning and preparing what your daughter eats each day. Plan a day's menu.

Is the menu varied? Does it contain foods from the five major food groups? Have you fed your girl enough? Remember, she's growing and energetic, so she needs lots of vitamins and nutrients throughout the day. Did you feed her enough milk and dairy products to support her growing bones? How about snacks? She'll probably get hungry between lunch and dinner, especially if she likes to play and run around. Are the snacks loaded with salt and sugar? Kids do tend to like sweets, and it's okay to include these in your daughter's menu as long as she's getting plenty of "power" nourishment, too.

Your daughter traipses downstairs before school and wants to skip breakfast. What do you do?

You might say something like this: "Even though you don't feel hungry, honey, your body still needs fuel first thing in the morning. Eating breakfast helps to jump-start your day: You'll think and move better afterwards. If you skip breakfast, your body and brain both have to work harder than necessary to keep you going. How about a waffle?"

Your daughter refuses to eat a snack before gymnastics class, even though she gets hungry halfway through.

She might be afraid of "getting fat" if she eats an extra meal or snack. She might even think she's eating too many calories. Talk to her gymnastics teacher and ask her to reinforce this message: "It's important that girl athletes who are in training eat extra snacks to help build their stamina. A lot of girls get the false idea from magazine diets that they need to limit what they eat. But that idea is wrong. Growing girls need to eat to grow. And if you're an athlete, you need to eat even more because you're expending so much energy. Most kids need three meals a day and at least one good, healthy snack during the afternoon."

You and your daughter are in a hurry and stop at McDonald's. What's the best thing to order?

We live in the real world where we sometimes have to grab food on the run. Even in these less-than-ideal situations, you can make healthy choices. Order the small fries, not the large. Salads aren't necessarily the healthiest way to go if you put on a ton of creamy dressing. It might be healthier to have a hamburger with mustard and ketchup. Red meat can be a good source of protein. And chicken, if broiled, is delicious and nutritious. It's less nutritious if fried.

Your daughter's gaining unneeded weight. She goes to her best friend's house each day after school. They snack on junk food all afternoon—foods high in sugar and fat but low in nutrition, like candy bars, chips, and ice cream.

Recall the difference between "power foods" and "junk foods." You can explain these differences to the girls themselves: "Eating junk food can make you tired, so you're more likely to eat and veg out on the couch and watch TV than ride a bike, go rollerblading, or kick a soccer ball." Also talk to the mom in the other house, express your concern, and make a few suggestions: "It can be hard to wean kids off junk foods, but this is easier to do if the families support each other. Let's have the kids prepare healthy snacks together such as skewers of fruit or trail mix with nuts they like."

"Ice cream makes you FAT!" your daughter exclaims.

You might respond like this: "That would be true—if you did *nothing* but eat ice cream your entire life! Every now and then, ice cream is good for you. It contains milk and calcium, which your bones and body need. You're so active, sweetheart, your body will burn up the ice cream and put it to good use. What flavor do you want to try?"

Unit Seven:
Feeding Our Many Appetites

ACTIVITIES

Core Activities
>   Action Check-In
>   Emotional Hunger: What's Eating You?
>   Two-Minute Meditation
>   Two-Minute Freewrite
>   Menu of Hungers
>   Call to Action Assignment
>   Closing Circle

Supplementary Activity
>   Yoga Primer 3: Finding Balance

OBJECTIVES

- To learn how to identify and respond to emotional and other "hungers" requiring nourishment other than food
- To identify effective ways to reduce stress
- To practice tuning into physical cues that signal stress and accompanying emotions
- To learn the basics of meditation to help calm the mind and body

MATERIALS AND PREPARATION

- ☐ Provide healthy snacks and beverages.
- ☐ Photocopy one "Menu of Hungers" (H-7A) per girl.
- ☐ Photocopy one "Call to Action" (H-7B) per girl.

CORE ACTIVITIES

Ground-Rule Review

⊃ Ask the girls to review the ground rules from memory. What's their sense: Are ground rules still needed?

Healthy Comment

⊃ Casually comment on the nutritional benefits of each snack. For example, "Strawberries and pineapple are great to eat when you're feeling stressed out. They're loaded with vitamin C, a natural stress reliever. The folic acid in these whole-wheat crackers is a powerful brain food."

⊃ Did the girls bring in "power" snacks to share? If so, invite them to comment on their provided food.

Action Check-In
(Time Estimate: 10 minutes)

⊃ Call on girls to report on each of the actions from Unit 6, reserving most of the time to review the investigation of school nutrition.

1. Did anyone create a beautiful mealtime this week? What did you do? Did it make a difference?
2. Anybody go shopping and get some new snacks?
3. What's up with the food in our school? Is it healthy and powerful?

⊃ Decide as a group what to do with the findings. Possible actions: Write an article for the school newspaper, schedule a meeting with the principal and the head of food services, prepare a presentation for the next PTA meeting, raise the issue at a student council meeting. Set deadlines, divvy up responsibilities, and arrange for another time to meet to follow through on determined action steps.

Emotional Hunger: What's Eating You?
(Time Estimate: 15 minutes)

⊃ Sample introduction:

" In our last group, we talked about how to feed our bodies. Today we're going to look at other appetites we sometimes overlook—or confuse with hunger for food. A big one is *emotional hunger*."

⊃ Pose a series of questions about stress:

1. Do your lives ever get stressful?
2. What kinds of things and situations tend to stress you out the most?
3. Where do you feel stress in your body?
4. How do you typically deal with stress?
5. Have any of you ever tried to cope by eating (or not eating)? Can someone give an example?
6. Can anyone explain the connection between food and stress?

⊃ Explain the connection between food and stress, as needed:

" When we were tiny babies and started to cry or fuss, our mothers would pick us up, hold us, coo to us—and often, feed us. When you're a mom, it's hard to tell if your baby needs *holding* or *feeding* because the cries sound the same. Now that we're grown up, it can still be hard to know if we need food or holding. The connection between emotional distress and eating is always in us. Some people, when they're feeling very emotional, eat more. Others forget to eat at all.

Everyone overeats, undereats, or turns to 'comfort foods' now and then. In some situations, eating might seem like the best and quickest way to calm ourselves down. There's a physiological reason for this. Carbohydrates raise our serotonin levels: They change our brain chemistry and numb us out. Eating is one way to comfort ourselves that might work in the short run. But what about the long run?

Eating to deal with painful feelings doesn't take away the real source of the pain. Over time, if we continue to avoid our emotions, we become disconnected from ourselves and what we need to feel safe and strong. In the long run, stuffing our feelings can cause us to feel powerless and depressed—and to develop an unhealthy relationship to food. If we get in the habit of eating whenever we're upset, we can gain weight."

⊃ Write the following headings across the top of the board:

NERVOUS   ANGRY   HAPPY

⊃ Comment before proceeding to the three scenarios: "Our own *bodies* are the first to tell us when we're under a lot of stress. That's why we've been practicing so many body scans and guided meditations—to help us tune in and listen."

⊃ Read each scenario aloud and write the girls' answers under the appropriate heading.

1. Everyone close your eyes and recall a situation where you felt really nervous—say, right before a big test.

   • What cues does your *body* give you to tell you you're nervous? Everyone let your body show your nervousness. Adopt a posture, make a movement, or let your face express nervousness. If anyone wants to move to another spot in the room, that's fine.
   • What does nervousness feel like in your body? Where, exactly, do you feel it?
   • What can help calm you down—other than eating?

2. Close your eyes again, and this time visualize a situation when you felt really angry—say, you found out that someone told a lie about you.

   • Notice how anger feels in your body and let your body express anger. Adopt a posture, make a movement, or let your face express anger.
   • Where do you feel anger in your body? What cues does your body give you?
   • What can help when you're angry—other than eating?

3. Close your eyes and remember a situation where you felt really happy.

   • Adopt a posture, make a movement, or let your face express happiness.
   • How does happiness feel inside your body? Where do you feel it the most?
   • What are ways to express or celebrate happiness—other than eating?

⊃ Sample answers:

Nervous	Happy	Angry
knee jumps	light	jittery
heart pounds	energized	sick
chew hair	chatty	hot face
sweaty pits	say hi to strangers	sulk
butterflies	laugh	clenched fists
What helps	*What helps*	*What helps*
deep breaths	smile	punch pillow
walk/exercise	dance	talk it out
talk to someone	sing	yell
go to bathroom		slam doors

Two-Minute Meditation
(Time Estimate: 5 minutes)

⊃ Pose the following questions:

" How many of you have heard this advice: 'When you're really mad, stop and take 10 deep breaths, counting backwards from 10 to 1'? Have any of you ever taken this advice? Can anybody guess why this is effective?"

⊃ Explain that this technique is a simplified form of meditation. Give details, as needed:

" Has anyone practiced formal meditation? When we're stressed out, our minds tend to rev up and go into overdrive. Some people call this agitated state 'monkey mind'. Can you guess why? Our minds swing this way and that, and jump all around, just like chattering monkeys swinging from tree to tree.

This mind-set doesn't help us one bit. In fact, it tends to aggravate the situation. What's needed during stressful times is a clear, calm mind that can stay one step removed from the problem—like a still lake at sunrise.

Meditation is one way to quiet the monkey mind. Just like those 10 simple breaths, meditation directs the mind to a single, simple focus. Some people meditate by closing their eyes and simply focusing on the *breath itself*, each inhale and ex-hale. When the mind wanders, you just notice that it has wandered and gently bring your attention back to your breath. Other people meditate by focusing on a *single word*, like 'peace' or 'shalom' or 'courage.' You can repeat this one word over and over in synch with your breathing. You can also fo-cus on a *meaningful sentence*, like one of the state-ments from the 'Full of Ourselves Proclamation' we learned in the first session."

◯ Ask each girl to decide on a single word, an im-age of a peaceful place, or a single sentence from the proclamation to use as her "mantra" and to write this down on the top of a journal page.

◯ Try a 2-minute meditation. Ask girls to find a comfortable place to lie down or to sit cross-legged with a straight spine. Read the directions aloud:

" Close your eyes and take a few long smooth breaths . . . As you breath in, notice your belly ex-pand. As you exhale, notice how your belly sinks . . . Now gently begin to focus on your image or repeat your mantra to yourself in your mind, in rhythm with each in-breath and each out-breath . . . Focus your attention on this simple man-tra, repeated in rhythm with your breathing . . . Whenever your mind wanders to another thought, simply *notice*—note to yourself 'thinking, think-ing'—then gently bring your attention and focus back to your mantra and your breathing . . . Try this for 2 minutes . . . I'll let you know when 2 minutes are up.

[At the end of 2 minutes]: "Notice how slowly you breathe when you are relaxed. Even your heart beats more slowly . . . Now gently deepen your breath . . . Wiggle your fingers and toes . . . Stretch your arms and legs in any way that feels

comfortable to you . . . Now open your eyes and notice how you feel."

◯ Proceed directly to the "Two-Minute Freewrite." Debrief both activities afterwards.

Two-Minute Freewrite
(Time Estimate: 5 minutes)

◯ Ask the girls to return to the journal page con-taining their mantra and explain the assignment:

" During meditation, as we grow quiet inside, it's possible to be aware of many things that the ordi-nary activity of the mind blocks out. This is an op-portune time to write in a journal. You don't have to know what you're going to say beforehand. Simply put your pen to paper—start with the mantra you wrote down earlier—and see what you have to say. You might reflect on the meaning of your mantra, or write a note to yourself, or sim-ply write down how you feel right now. Let's try writing for 2 minutes."

◯ Debriefing questions:

1. What was meditating like for you? Did your mind drift off your mantra? (This is normal. The point is to remain *aware*. If your mind wanders, simply be aware that it's wander-ing, and gently direct your attention back to the mantra. With practice, it gets easier to direct your focus.)
2. Would anyone like to share your freewrite?

Menu of Hungers
(Time Estimate: 15 minutes)

◯ Distribute and review the handout "Menu of Hungers" (H-7A). Sample introduction:

" We've figured out a lot of ways to satisfy emotional hungers. We have other hungers that deserve at-tention, too. Maybe we hunger for friendship or for alone time or for physical activity. At these times, it's really easy to grab something out of the fridge or rip open a bag of chips—since food represents quick satisfaction. But since our *bodies* aren't actu-ally hungry, no amount of food will satisfy."

⤳ Ask for a volunteer to read the introductory paragraph on the handout.

⤳ Review hungers one at a time. Draw from the questions below to help girls relate from their own experience.

1. Can anyone remember a time you felt really bored, like you were about to go out of your mind from boredom? This is *intellectual hunger*, and you need some "food for thought." Read down the list and check any items that you already try or that might make sense to try in the future. Then add three more things you do—or could try—to nourish this hunger.

2. Have you ever felt a hunger to move, a *physical hunger*? Can anyone tell about a time you felt all charged up, like your body could just burst out in movement? Read down the list and check any items you already try. Then add three more things you already do—or could try—to feed this hunger for movement.

3. What about loneliness? Can you recall a time you needed a friend and someone to talk to? Maybe you felt left out. Check any items you already try. Then add three more things you already do—or could try—to nourish this *friendship hunger*.

4. Was there ever a time you felt like you'd had way too much of people, when you were "fed up" with everyone and needed some space of your own? Read down the list and check any items you already try. Then add three more things you already do—or could try—to feed this *hunger for solitude*.

5. Can anyone describe a *spiritual hunger*? Have you ever felt the need to connect with a sense of purpose or with something bigger? Check any items you already try. Then add three more things you already do—or could try—to nourish this hunger for meaning.

6. Last is *creative hunger*. Can you recall a time when you felt inspired, when your creative energy was flowing and you needed to invent something new? What do you do with that kind of energy? Check any items you already try. Then add three more things you already do—or could try—to satisfy this hunger for invention.

⤳ Point out that these are all ways to nourish and take care of ourselves when our bodies aren't hungry but we need to be filled/fulfilled.

Call to Action Assignment
(Time Estimate: 4 minutes)

⤳ Hand out "Call to Action" sheets (H-7B) and review the assignments.

⤳ Answer any questions, and hold the girls accountable for reporting on their action steps at the start of the next session.

Closing Circle
(Time Estimate: 15 seconds)

⤳ Stand in a circle, join hands, and affirm in unison: "Together we make a difference, differences included."

SUPPLEMENTAL ACTIVITY

Yoga Primer 3: Finding Balance
(Time Estimate: 20 minutes)

⤳ Invite girls to try some basic yoga postures as a way to connect to an inner sense of balance and strength.

⤳ Turn to the "Yoga Primer" (Addendum A) and advance through the third sequence of discussion and postures:

Warm-Up Questions
Energetic Warm-Up: Wood Chopper
Warrior 1
Child Pose
Deep Relaxation

Unit Eight:
The Power of Healthy Relationships

ACTIVITIES

Core Activities

> Action Check-In
> The Human Mirror
> Constellation of Connection
> Case Studies: How Good Are You at Conflict?
> Popularity: A Discussion
> Keepsakes: A Wrap-Up
> Call to Action Contract
> Closing Circle

Supplemental Activities

> Take 1, Take 2: Connection Statues
> Celebratory Moms' Session
> Full of Ourselves Bulletin Board

OBJECTIVES

- To understand that relational health is a key aspect of overall well-being
- To recognize that healthy "connection," with oneself and others, is a source of strength
- To analyze how popularity affects relationships
- To practice conflict resolution
- To pledge to apply the Full of Ourselves principles in daily life
- To wrap up the first program phase and revisit session highlights

MATERIALS AND PREPARATION

- ☐ Provide healthy snacks and beverages.
- ☐ If affordable, buy roses or other sturdy flowers and give one to each girl at the end of this final Full of Ourselves session.
- ☐ Photocopy one "Constellation of Connection" (H-8A) per girl.
- ☐ Photocopy the "Conflict Case Studies" (H-8B) and cut the five case studies into separate strips.
- ☐ Make one copy of the "Call to Action Contract" (H-8C) per girl.

CORE ACTIVITIES

Healthy Comment

⟳ Comment casually about the nutritional benefits of each snack. For example, "Do any of you tire out easily? Try eating more 'orange foods' like these peach and papaya chunks, packed with vitamin A. Everyone help yourself to drinks. Can anyone guess how long a person can survive without fluids? Without water, we'd die in 3–5 *days!* Our bodies are about 70% water, so we need to rehydrate constantly."

Action Check-In
(Time Estimate: 5–10 minutes)

⟳ Call on girls to report on each of the actions from the last unit.

1. Tell us about your experience with meditation.
2. Tell us about your experience with journal writing.
3. Did you remember to check in with your "hungers"?
4. How do your parents and other adults deal with stress?

☞ *Teaching Note:* If the girls mention smoking or drinking or other potentially unhealthy habits, ask them to consider: "Are these *healthy* ways of coping?"

The Human Mirror
(Time Estimate: 5–10 minutes)

☞ *Teaching Note:* Don't skip this activity. It sets a wonderful stage for the "Constellation of Connection."

⟳ Demonstrate with a girl volunteer. Sit cross-legged on the floor, facing each other. Sit close enough that your knees nearly touch. You're the leader first. Hold up your hands in front of you, palms facing out toward your partner. She does the same, so that her hands "mirror" yours. Your sets of hands don't touch; leave several inches between them.

⟳ Explain that you will lead and she will be your "mirror image." Look each other in the eyes and,

without breaking gaze, her hands follow yours. The entire exercise is to be done in slow motion and without talking. Move one hand up toward the ceiling and down, to the right, to the left, and so on. Do the same with your opposite hand; then move both of your hands simultaneously, forward and back, in slow swooping arches, and so on.

⟳ Girls pair up and decide who will lead first. Direct girls to move very slowly, without talking, "as if you are moving through molasses." The goal is to move so perfectly in synch that a passerby wouldn't be able to tell who was the "reflection."

⟳ After each girl takes a turn as leader, wrap up in a manner like this:

❝ It's so beautiful to watch all of you. You look like you're doing an intricate dance—in relationship with each other. It can be a very powerful experience to be so in synch with another human being."

Constellation of Connection
(Time Estimate: 10 minutes)

⟳ Sample introduction:

❝ We've been talking a lot about how to take care of ourselves—how to care for and feed our bodies, how to respond to our emotions and other hungers, particularly when we're under stress. Another way we take care of ourselves is through our *relationships.* This unit is called 'The Power of Healthy Relationships.' Can anyone figure out how relationships make us powerful?"

⟳ Hand out "Constellation of Connection" (H-8A).

⟳ Instruct everyone to write their own name in the center circle: "Your most important relationship is with *yourself.* Does this make sense?"

⟳ In each of the remaining eight circles, ask girls to write down the name of a person to whom they feel connected:

❝ Take a minute to think about the people who are important in your life today: friends, family members of all ages, teachers, people you love, and people you struggle with. Struggle is a form of connection, too."

⊃ Ask the girls to consider each person in her constellation, one at a time: "How is your relationship with this person going right now?"

⊃ Direct the girls to draw lines from their central circle to each person in the constellation. The type of line they choose to draw will define the state of connection at *this point in time*. They can choose from three types of lines, each representing a different relational dynamic:

1. A double solid line indicates a *strong connection*. You are well connected.
2. A dash indicates that you'd like *more connection* with that person. For example, you talk to your grandma now and then, but you'd like to see her more.
3. A squiggle indicates that there is *tension and stress* in the relationship right now.

⊃ Discussion questions:

1. Consider your strongest relationships, those with the double line. What is it about these relationships that makes them the strongest?
2. Consider the people with whom you're struggling or to whom you'd like to be closer. How much *choice and power* do you have over the state of these relationships?

⊃ Ask the girls to write down in their journals the name of one person *with whom they'd like to have a stronger connection*. Below the name, have them list three things they can do to strengthen the relationship.

⊃ Ask for volunteers to describe the chosen relationship and actions that might lead to better connection.

⊃ Ask the girls to write their *own name* on the top of the next journal page. Say, "Underneath, list three things you can do to strengthen your connection with yourself." Ask for volunteers to share their ideas.

⊕ *Time Check:* If you have an extra 10 minutes, this is a good point to do the supplementary "Connection Statues" activity.

Case Studies:
How Good Are You at Conflict?
(Time Estimate: 15 minutes)

⊃ Pose a question to start: "Agree or disagree: The best relationships are free of conflict."

⊃ Reinforce, if needed:

" Conflict is an inevitable part of every relationship. If we know how to handle and work through conflict, it often leads to deeper understanding between two people. How well we deal with conflict is what makes the difference between healthy and unhealthy connection."

⊃ Divide the girls into groups of three. Give a different "Conflict Case Study" (H-8B) to each group. Allow groups a few minutes to discuss the conflict and come up with a healthy resolution.

" As you review your case, keep in mind the power of connection. See in each case whether it's possible to find a way to stay in connection with both *yourself* and *others* as you resolve the conflict."

⊃ Ask each group to present and debrief their case. Invite other girls to suggest alternative ways to resolve each scenario. During each presentation, pose two questions:

1. How important is connection here? With whom?
2. Is there room for compromise in this situation?

⊃ Point out, if needed:

" Your power comes from staying in connection—to yourself always, and to others, too, except when you're in danger or asked to sacrifice your values.
    If connection is important, then some degree of compromise will probably be needed to resolve the conflict. Give-and-take is important to keep relationships healthy—as long as you aren't asked to sacrifice your connection to yourself or your core values. Remember the personal values you defined in the unit on media literacy."

⊃ Specific debriefing points:

- Case 4: Why do some girls say things like this? Some girls and women try to bond through body loathing, but this is an unhealthy form of connection in which everyone involved loses. Putting ourselves down just brings us *all* down! We give power to whatever we focus on, so if we focus on what's *wrong* with us, we wind up feeling worse. On the contrary, if we focus on what's *right* with us, we wind up feeling more confident and powerful.

- Case 5: We each get to *choose* whether or not we want to connect with someone. If anybody threatens you or asks you to compromise yourself in a big way, get away from him or her and disconnect immediately! In a situation like this, it doesn't matter what other people think. All that matters is that you take care of *you*.

Popularity: A Discussion
(Time Estimate: 10 minutes)

⊃ Discussion questions:

1. How does popularity affect your relationships? Has there ever been a time when you were untrue to yourself—when you said or did something that didn't feel quite right to you, that wasn't quite "you"—in order to be more popular?
2. What *is* popularity anyway? Who gets to decide who is and isn't popular?

⊃ Ask the girls to return to the "Full of Ourselves Proclamation" (taped in their journals), read through the statements, and star two ideas they'd like to remember the next time they're tempted to compromise themselves.

⊃ Go around the circle: "Which ideas did you choose?"

Keepsakes: A Wrap-Up
(Time Estimate: 5 minutes)

⊃ Ask the girls to reflect back on their experience in the group.

" What do you want to take with you from our group? What do you want to be sure you never forget? This could be anything—a big or small idea, something someone said, or something that happened during a session."

⊃ Ask everyone to write down in their journals two or three things they want to remember. Ask for volunteers to share.

⊃ Sample wrap-up:

" We've talked all these weeks about how to stay connected to ourselves, to our bodies, and to others in positive and powerful ways. We've also talked about things that can get in the way of connection, like prejudice and weightism and unhealthy messages in the media. I've watched you all grow and become more confident and powerful during this time. I've watched you deepen your connections to yourselves and to one another. Together we really do make a difference in the world—and now you're ready to be leaders, to take what we've learned and to pass it on to other girls."

Call to Action Contract
(Time Estimate: 5 minutes)

⊃ Give one "Call to Action Contract" (H-8C) to each girl. Ask girls to read the contract and see if there are other "intentions" they'd like to add.

⊃ Remind the girls of the "Tree of Strength" activity and all of the powerful qualities they identified in themselves and in the women in their lives. This is what is meant by being "full of ourselves"—in the best sense of the phrase.

⊃ Invite everyone to read the contract in unison and sign each other's sheets as witnesses.

Closing Circle
(Time Estimate: 15 seconds)

⊃ Stand in a circle, join hands, and declare in unison: "Together we make a difference, differences included."

PROCEED TO THROW YOUR WEIGHT AROUND

⊃ Fill girls in on details about Throw Your Weight Around, the mentoring phase of the program. During your first planning session, give each girl a copy of *Throw Your Weight Around! A Guide for Girl Leaders*.

⊃ Proceed to *Throw Your Weight Around! A Guide for Adult Leaders*.

SUPPLEMENTAL ACTIVITIES

Take 1, Take 2: Connection Statues
(Time Estimate: 15 minutes)

⊃ Clear a space big enough for the girls to move around.

⊃ Girls work in trios. One girl volunteers to be the "sculptor," and the other two girls are her "actors."

⊃ The sculptor will sculpt her actors into two "statues." Review the directions with sculptors:

1. Choose one person from your "Constellation of Connection" with whom you'd like to have a better relationship.
2. Designate one actor to be "you" and the other to be the person identified from your constellation.
3. Decide on a pose your actors should assume to represent the *current* state of your relationship with this person. For example, if you don't feel heard in the relationship right now, you might have one actor clamp her hands down over her ears while the other actor pretends to be talking. Once you've "sculpted" the relationship, actors freeze in their places so that you can make minor adjustments to their arms, facial expressions, and postures.

Be sure their pose is exactly as you like. Actors should memorize this pose and be able to repeat it.
4. Think of a title for this first "sculpture."
5. Now set up a second statue representing how you'd ideally *like* the relationship between you and your chosen person to be. Again, direct actors into their places, making sure their postures and expressions suit you. Actors should be able to assume this pose later when asked.
6. Think of a title for this second sculpture.

⊃ Ask each sculptor to introduce her actors to the group; for example, "This is me, this is my brother." The sculptor then directs her actors into the two statues: "Title 1 . . . Title 2 . . ."

Celebratory Moms' Session
(Time Estimate: 1 planning session, 1 group session)

⊃ Find out if the girls are interested in holding a special session for their moms or other adult women who are important to them (aunts, grandmothers, next-door neighbors).

⊃ Set a day and time and design invitations for girls to hand-deliver to their moms and/or other women.

⊃ Hold a planning session. Help girls decide on five or six favorite activities from the program to try with their moms. Ask girls to volunteer individually or in pairs to facilitate activities. Photocopy activities from the curriculum for girls to rehearse. Sample session outline:

Welcome

FOO Brainstorm (Unit 1)

Tree of Strength (Unit 2)

Conscious Eating (Unit 6)

10 Beautiful Things (Unit 5)

Yoga: Warrior 1 (Unit 2)

Hi, Body (Unit 5)

Closing Circle (every unit)

⊃ Reserve the school library or another special room for the session. Create a beautiful setting with flowers and food; ask if any girls would like to bake for the occasion. As an art project, girls can create tissue paper flower bouquets.

⊃ If the session is a success, consider planning a second one exclusively for dads and/or other important men in girls' lives.

Full of Ourselves Bulletin Board
(Time Estimate: Ongoing project)

⊃ Reserve a large public bulletin board and ask girls to design and install a "Full of Ourselves" display to publicize the program to the rest of the community.

⊃ Help girls organize the project:

1. Decide on information to highlight. What particulars about the program and their experience would girls like to share with others (e.g., who, what, why, how)?
2. Lay out the design.
3. Gather necessary materials: colored paper, scissors, stapler, and so on.
4. Arrange times to complete the installation.
5. Photograph the board for your archives.

⊃ If you'll be working with younger girls in the same building during program phase 2, show them the board and add their names or pictures to the display.

Full of Ourselves Proclamation

Photocopy and cut out one square per participant.

★ **Full of Ourselves Proclamation** ★

A girl who is full of herself, in the best sense of the phrase, might say 10 things like this:

- I know who I am.
- I know that *I* matter.
- I know what matters to me.
- I pay attention to what I feel and what I need.
- I make choices and decisions that are good for me.
- I take good care of my body.
- I stand up for what I believe in.
- I let people know what I think, even when I'm angry or confused or in disagreement with everyone else.
- I am a valuable friend.
- I know I can make a positive difference in the world in my own unique way.

★ **Full of Ourselves Proclamation** ★

A girl who is full of herself, in the best sense of the phrase, might say 10 things like this:

- I know who I am.
- I know that *I* matter.
- I know what matters to me.
- I pay attention to what I feel and what I need.
- I make choices and decisions that are good for me.
- I take good care of my body.
- I stand up for what I believe in.
- I let people know what I think, even when I'm angry or confused or in disagreement with everyone else.
- I am a valuable friend.
- I know I can make a positive difference in the world in my own unique way.

★ **Full of Ourselves Proclamation** ★

A girl who is full of herself, in the best sense of the phrase, might say 10 things like this:

- I know who I am.
- I know that *I* matter.
- I know what matters to me.
- I pay attention to what I feel and what I need.
- I make choices and decisions that are good for me.
- I take good care of my body.
- I stand up for what I believe in.
- I let people know what I think, even when I'm angry or confused or in disagreement with everyone else.
- I am a valuable friend.
- I know I can make a positive difference in the world in my own unique way.

★ **Full of Ourselves Proclamation** ★

A girl who is full of herself, in the best sense of the phrase, might say 10 things like this:

- I know who I am.
- I know that *I* matter.
- I know what matters to me.
- I pay attention to what I feel and what I need.
- I make choices and decisions that are good for me.
- I take good care of my body.
- I stand up for what I believe in.
- I let people know what I think, even when I'm angry or confused or in disagreement with everyone else.
- I am a valuable friend.
- I know I can make a positive difference in the world in my own unique way.

Call to Action
Unit 1: Full of Ourselves

Action is the test of our success. Let's demonstrate our commitment to ourselves, to one another, and to making a positive difference in the world.

★ Personal Action ★

1. Read the Full of Ourselves Proclamation aloud to yourself every day.

Say each statement like you mean it! See if you can memorize the proclamation by the next group session.

I know who I am. I know that I matter. I know what matters to me. I pay attention to what I feel and what I need. I make choices and decisions that are good for me. I take good care of my body. I stand up for what I believe in. I let people know what I think, even when I'm angry or confused or in disagreement with everyone else. I am a valuable friend. I know I can make a positive difference in the world in my own unique way.

2. Every day, take a few minutes to check in with your body.

Sit or lie down, close your eyes, and take a few long breaths. Notice your belly as it rises and falls with each breath. Notice how your body is feeling: energetic, calm, sluggish, warm, or cool. Are you feeling any particular emotion? Now let your attention slowly travel from the top of your head down through the tips of your toes like a long wave of golden light. Imagine that you are inhaling light through every pore of your skin. This light fills you with inner confidence and power. As you breathe, notice the sensation of power and light throughout your entire body.

★ Action at Home ★

3. Informal interview #1.

Ask your mom or another adult woman to tell you about a time she felt really confident and powerful. If she needs a little time to think about it, that's fine. Be sure to check back with her later.

4. Informal interview #2.

Ask at least two adult family members (or other grown-ups who know you well) to tell you about a time they felt really proud of *you*.

★ Action in the World ★

5. Get brave about being yourself.

Try to speak your mind this week—confidently and respectfully—especially in situations where you might be tempted to hold back and silence yourself. Be ready to report how this feels. Even if it's really hard and you don't speak up, come back and tell us about how that felt.

"Tree of Strength" Leaves

Call to Action
Unit 2: Claiming Our Strengths

> Action is the test of our success. Let's demonstrate our commitment to ourselves, to one another, and to making a positive difference in the world.

★ Personal Action ★

1. Practice positive self-talk!

Be your own best friend. Whenever you're feeling down or doubtful, give yourself encouragement.

2. Take positive steps toward your stated goal.

In the "Learning to Walk" activity, you identified a goal you want to reach in the next few days or weeks. Take at least one action toward your goal and see what results.

3. Write a gratitude list.

List 10 things you are grateful for in your life right now. These can include everything from specific friends and family members to the ability to hear the sound of rain.

★ Action at Home ★

4. Add two new leaves to the Tree of Strength!

Interview two adult family members. Ask each one to tell you about a woman he or she admires and why. Come prepared to add these women to the Tree of Strength.

★ Action in the World ★

5. Let a "powerful woman" know that you admire her.

Choose one of your five "powerful women" and tell her in person (or over the phone or via e-mail) what she means to you. If she's no longer alive, write a note or a letter and read it to the moon.

6. Be brave about being yourself!

Try to put these statements from the proclamation into action: "I stand up for what I believe in. I let people know what I think, even when I'm angry or confused or in disagreement with everyone else." Be ready to talk about this in the next meeting.

Fat Myths

Cut the following statements into separate strips and put in a paper "grab bag."

★ Body fat is bad; it serves no good purpose on anyone's body.

★ The thinnest girl in the room is the happiest girl in the room.

★ People get fat because they eat too much and exercise too little.

★ The thinner you are, the healthier you are.

Group Pledge

Photocopy and cut out one square for each girl.

★ I vow to do my best to *understand*, *respect*, and *include* other people, no matter what they look like. Humans come in *all* shapes, colors, and sizes!

★ I vow to do my best to *understand*, *respect*, and *include* other people, no matter what they look like. Humans come in *all* shapes, colors, and sizes!

★ I vow to do my best to *understand*, *respect*, and *include* other people, no matter what they look like. Humans come in *all* shapes, colors, and sizes!

★ I vow to do my best to *understand*, *respect*, and *include* other people, no matter what they look like. Humans come in *all* shapes, colors, and sizes!

★ I vow to do my best to *understand*, *respect*, and *include* other people, no matter what they look like. Humans come in *all* shapes, colors, and sizes!

★ I vow to do my best to *understand*, *respect*, and *include* other people, no matter what they look like. Humans come in *all* shapes, colors, and sizes!

★ I vow to do my best to *understand*, *respect*, and *include* other people, no matter what they look like. Humans come in *all* shapes, colors, and sizes!

★ I vow to do my best to *understand*, *respect*, and *include* other people, no matter what they look like. Humans come in *all* shapes, colors, and sizes!

★ I vow to do my best to *understand*, *respect*, and *include* other people, no matter what they look like. Humans come in *all* shapes, colors, and sizes!

★ I vow to do my best to *understand*, *respect*, and *include* other people, no matter what they look like. Humans come in *all* shapes, colors, and sizes!

Call to Action
Unit 3: Body Politics

> Action is the test of our success. Let's demonstrate our commitment to ourselves, to one another, and to making a positive difference in the world.

★ Personal Action ★

1. Read the Group Pledge aloud to yourself every day.

Take it to heart. Think about what it means to be a leader and take a stand against prejudice in your daily life. Try to memorize the pledge by the next group session.

I vow to do my best to understand, respect, and include other people, no matter what they look like. Humans come in all shapes, colors, and sizes!

★ Action at Home ★

2. Informal interview.

Ask your mom or another adult woman to tell you about three things she really likes and appreciates about her body and physical capabilities.

★ Action in the World ★

3. Be a social scientist: Stay on the lookout for "body messages."

Play detective and search for "body messages and behaviors" in the world. Notice the ways people treat one another based on the size and shape of their bodies. Be sure to note positive body messages as well as negative ones.

For example, listen to the ways girls and boys talk about bodies. Is there a difference? Who "body talks" more? Pay attention to what grown-ups say about bodies—their own and others'. Watch for body messages on TV and at the movies. Listen for body talk in songs. How are large women and girls portrayed? How about small men and boys? Are tall people treated differently than short ones? Are girls with big chests treated differently than girls with smaller ones?

Carry a pad at all times so you can document your findings. Write down the "body talk" you hear and the "body behaviors" you notice. Try not to use names! And remember: The point isn't to snoop on others. It's to raise your own awareness so you're in a better position to choose what you want to say and do in response to bad body messages.

Quick Comebacks

Photocopy and cut into separate strips. Each girl gets one copy of each script.

★ Comeback 1: Shoes ★

HARASSER [grabbing at shoe]: I want that shoe! Give it to me!

TARGET: No, it's mine. You can't have it.

★ Comeback 2: Eyes ★

HARASSER: Your eyes are _____! (false statement)

TARGET: No, that's not true. My eyes are _____.

You're wrong. My eyes are _____.

★ Comeback 3: Shirt ★

HARASSER: Your shirt is really ugly! (opinion)

TARGET: That's your opinion. I really like it.

I can't believe you just said that. What a rude thing to say!

Your comment is really ugly.

That really hurts my feelings.

The Cafeteria

One day Angela and her friend Hayley are eating lunch together in the cafeteria. They're sitting at a long table with a bunch of other students. The two girls are in the middle of a conversation when Sam and his pal Peter walk by with their lunch trays.

While passing by, Sam stops and stares at Angela's plate and comments just loudly enough for the girls to hear: "What a cow!"

Angela's face turns red.

Then Peter pipes in: "Shouldn't you go on a diet or something?" he asks in a nasty tone of voice.

Angela is clearly upset. Hayley feels badly but doesn't know what to do.

The Party: A Scene for Three Characters and a Narrator

NARRATOR: A bunch of girls are sitting at the lunch table, talking excitedly.

ALICE: Fionna, I'm *so* excited about your party tomorrow night! I can't wait!

LILLY: Me, too! Who did you invite?

FIONNA: Everybody! Peter, Jarvis, Danny, Alex . . .

ALICE: What about girls?

LILLY: You didn't invite Jennifer, did you?

FIONNA: Of course not! I don't want to be associated with her. She's so *fat*!

LILLY: Yeah, she'd probably just hang around the table and eat everything in sight.

ALICE: Wait a minute, you guys. We were all hanging out at Jennifer's last weekend.

FIONNA: Yeah, but so what? That was just *girls*. This is my first big party and I don't want anybody fat or bad or ugly to spoil it. I want it to be *perfect*.

LILLY: Fionna's right. None of the boys like Jennifer. They think she's gross.

NARRATOR: No one else speaks up. You're at the table, too. What do you say or do?

The Party: Assigned Roles

Photocopy and cut out squares

★ *"Just because the boys make fun of Jennifer doesn't mean that we should. Think about it: We don't have to stoop to their low level."*

You're a good friend of Jennifer's. You're also an **activist**: a girl who has a keen and strong sense of fairness. You hate it when anyone is treated unfairly. You're courageous enough to speak out even when everyone else has a different opinion.

★ *"I don't know Jen very well since I'm new here, but I think it shouldn't matter what somebody looks like. It's what kind of person they are that counts."*

You're a new girl at school, so you don't know Jennifer very well—or any of the other girls. You're also an **activist**: a girl with a keen and strong sense of fairness. You hate it when anyone is treated unfairly.

★ *"Fionna, I think you're absolutely right. You shouldn't let somebody like Jennifer ruin your party."*

You're dying to be Fionna's friend, but she doesn't like you at all. You'll do anything to get her to like you, even if it means being cruel to Jennifer. You're a **follower**.

★ *"You guys, you're being really mean. Imagine if Jen were here and heard all this. What does it matter how big she is? I think she's really nice, and she's fun to have around."*

Jennifer is your best friend, so you can't stand what Fionna is saying about her. You're also an **activist** with a keen and strong sense of fairness. You hate it when anyone is treated unfairly.

★ *"I wouldn't invite Jennifer to my party either!"*

You're dying to go to Fionna's party. You'll do or say anything to get an invitation. You're a **follower**.

★ *"Jennifer's a loser. Did you see the shirt she was wearing today? It's embarrassing!"*

You are an **instigator**, like Fionna. You like to gossip about others and stir up trouble. Since Jennifer doesn't like you at all, you're thrilled to attack her with everyone else.

★ *"Lilly's right. Nobody likes fat people. Do we really want to be friends with her?"*

You're a good friend of Fionna's and you're an **instigator**, just like her. You love turning girls against one another just for the fun of it.

★ *"Fionna, you know I'm your best friend. But how would you feel if somebody did this to you?"*

You're best friends with Fionna and Lilly. You're also an **activist** with a keen and strong sense of fairness. You hate it when anyone is treated unfairly.

★ *"Fionna, you know that Jennifer and I don't get along. She isn't my friend or anything. But, still, I wouldn't disinvite her to my party just because of her body size. That's wrong. What if you gain weight someday and somebody does this to you?"*

You don't like Jennifer. But you're also an **activist**: a girl who has a keen and strong sense of fairness. You hate it when anyone is treated unfairly. You're courageous enough to speak out even when everyone else has a different opinion.

★ *"You've got a bad attitude, Fionna. I know what this feels like—because you've done this to me before. It stinks."*

You can't stand Fionna's attitude. She has bullied and excluded you in the past. You're an **activist** with a keen and strong sense of fairness. You hate it when anyone is treated unfairly.

★ *"You guys, I can't believe you're saying these things! How can you be so cruel?"*

You're a very popular girl. What you say matters in this group. You're also an **activist**: someone who has a keen and strong sense of fairness. You hate it when anyone is treated unfairly.

★ *"I think Jennifer's gross, too. I wouldn't invite her to my party either."*

You're an unpopular girl and want to be liked. You're scared to stand up for Jennifer. You're a **follower** who goes along with the crowd.

The Wall

NARRATOR: It's Friday afternoon. School's over for the week. Three 8th-grade boys named Connor, Rashad, and Luke are sitting together on a wall talking and joking around. Lauren, a 7th grader, is walking home from school and happens to pass by in front of them.

CONNOR [loudly enough so Lauren can hear]: "5."

RASHAD [obnoxious]: You've gotta be kidding! "4." Look at those thunder thighs.

LUKE: She's flat as a board. I give her a "3."

LAUREN: [Says nothing, but her body language shows how uncomfortable she feels.]

NARRATOR: FREEZE!

Call to Action
Unit 4: Standing Our Ground

> Action is the test of our success. Let's demonstrate our commitment to ourselves, to one another, and to making a positive difference in the world.

★ Personal Action ★

1. Continue to read the Group Pledge aloud to yourself every day.

Take it to heart. Think about what it means to be a leader and to take action against prejudice in your daily life.

I do my best to understand, respect, and include other people, no matter what they look like. Humans come in all shapes, colors, and sizes!

★ Action at Home ★

2. Interview two adults about activism.

Ask them to tell you about a time in their lives when they stood up for themselves or for someone else who was being treated unfairly. What did they say or do? What happened as a result? If they can't think of an example, ask them to tell you about a time they *wished* they'd had the courage to take a stand.

★ Action in the World ★

3. Be an activist!

Whenever you hear anyone being teased, excluded, or put down for the way they look, don't buy in. Instead, speak up. Try a comeback: "That's mean" or "You're wrong" or "I can't believe you just said/did that!"

Full of Ourselves, Copyright © 2006 by Teachers College, Columbia University

Values Squares

Personality	Pretty Face	Great Hair
Self-Respect	Animals	Nature
Self-Expression	Solving Problems	Sexiness
Honesty	Courage	Shopping
Boyfriend/Cute Guys	Respect from Others	Good Food
Music	Spirituality	Athletic Ability
Popularity	Great Body	Sense of Humor
Talents and Hobbies	TV and Movies	Health
Loyalty	Good Grades	Clothes
Friendships	Family	Intelligence
Love	Creativity	Leadership

Magazines: What's Up

Photocopy and cut out one square for each pair of girls.

★ **Fashion Magazines: What's Up?** ★

Find an article or photo that is about a girl or woman leader.

★ **Fashion Magazines: What's Up?** ★

How many total pages are in your magazine? How many of these pages are advertisements?

★ **Fashion Magazines: What's Up?** ★

Look around this room at the range of body types. Try to find the same range of body shapes and sizes and colors in your magazines. Are all of these body types associated with *good* things?

★ **Fashion Magazines: What's Up?** ★

Find an article or photo showing girls or women *doing* something extraordinary or exciting.

★ **Fashion Magazines: What's Up?** ★

Find an article or photograph that is about eating and enjoying yummy food.

★ **Fashion Magazines: What's Up?** ★

Find three photographs that are about sexiness and getting attention from boys or men.

★ **Fashion Magazines: What's Up?** ★

Look through the photos of female models. Which pose looks most ridiculous or uncomfortable? Try holding this pose for 2 minutes.

★ **Fashion Magazines: What's Up?** ★

How many articles and ads can you find that tell females how to change, fix, or improve their bodies? How many articles and ads can you find about self-acceptance?

★ **Fashion Magazines: What's Up?** ★

Look through the photographs. Count the number of big-boned or big-bodied girls. How are they portrayed (happy/unhappy, popular/unpopular)?

★ **Fashion Magazines: What's Up?** ★

Find an article or photograph that is about girls or women joining together to help each other out or to make a difference in the world.

Full of Ourselves, Copyright © 2006 by Teachers College, Columbia University

"Hi, Body" Affirmation

Photocopy and cut out one square for each girl.

Hi, Body!

You are going to carry me through this day. Because of you, I can dance, I can see, I can taste, I can sing, I can kiss. With your help, I can show the world who I am today. I will take really good care of you because you are my only body. And as I love and respect you, you'll take good care of me. We are allies; you stand up for me and I stand up for you, no matter what anyone else says. We'll be friends through thick and thin. We're friends for life.

Hi, Body!

You are going to carry me through this day. Because of you, I can dance, I can see, I can taste, I can sing, I can kiss. With your help, I can show the world who I am today. I will take really good care of you because you are my only body. And as I love and respect you, you'll take good care of me. We are allies; you stand up for me and I stand up for you, no matter what anyone else says. We'll be friends through thick and thin. We're friends for life.

Hi, Body!

You are going to carry me through this day. Because of you, I can dance, I can see, I can taste, I can sing, I can kiss. With your help, I can show the world who I am today. I will take really good care of you because you are my only body. And as I love and respect you, you'll take good care of me. We are allies; you stand up for me and I stand up for you, no matter what anyone else says. We'll be friends through thick and thin. We're friends for life.

Hi, Body!

You are going to carry me through this day. Because of you, I can dance, I can see, I can taste, I can sing, I can kiss. With your help, I can show the world who I am today. I will take really good care of you because you are my only body. And as I love and respect you, you'll take good care of me. We are allies; you stand up for me and I stand up for you, no matter what anyone else says. We'll be friends through thick and thin. We're friends for life.

Hi, Body!

You are going to carry me through this day. Because of you, I can dance, I can see, I can taste, I can sing, I can kiss. With your help, I can show the world who I am today. I will take really good care of you because you are my only body. And as I love and respect you, you'll take good care of me. We are allies; you stand up for me and I stand up for you, no matter what anyone else says. We'll be friends through thick and thin. We're friends for life.

Hi, Body!

You are going to carry me through this day. Because of you, I can dance, I can see, I can taste, I can sing, I can kiss. With your help, I can show the world who I am today. I will take really good care of you because you are my only body. And as I love and respect you, you'll take good care of me. We are allies; you stand up for me and I stand up for you, no matter what anyone else says. We'll be friends through thick and thin. We're friends for life.

Call to Action
Unit 5: Countering the Media Culture

Action is the test of our success. Let's demonstrate our commitment to ourselves, to one another, and to making a positive difference in the world.

★ Personal Action ★

1. **Read the "Hi, Body" affirmation aloud to yourself every day.**

   Take time each day to appreciate all the things your body allows you to do. Feel free to change words and add ideas of your own.

   Hi, Body. You are going to carry me through this day. Because of you, I can dance, I can see, I can taste, I can sing, I can kiss. With your help, I can show the world who I am today. I will take really good care of you because you are my only body. And as I love and respect you, you'll take good care of me. We are allies; you stand up for me and I stand up for you, no matter what anyone else says. We'll be friends through thick and thin. We're friends for life.

2. **Remember your list of 10 beautiful things? Make these part of your everyday life.**

   Surround yourself with words, images, and things that make you feel inspired. Post your list on the inside of your locker, decorate a bulletin board with pictures of your beautiful things, or clear off a tabletop and create a "shrine" to help keep you connected with what you truly find beautiful. For example, if your list included seashells, pinecones, and your grandmother, place shells and cones on the table along with your grandmother's picture.

★ Action at Home ★

3. **Take a close look at all the magazines in your home.**

   Notice how you feel after reading each one. Do you feel *better* or *worse* about yourself? If worse, take a personal stand and decide not to buy or read that magazine! Explain to your parents or other adult family members why you've made this decision, and invite them to join in your boycott.

★ Action in the World ★

4. **Talk back!**

   You can take this action on your own or with friends. Take another look at your fashion magazine. Is there anything you'd like to say to the publisher or to one of the advertisers? Does anything make you mad? Is there a particular article or an advertisement that is "unfriendly" to girls and young women? Send an e-mail or a letter to the magazine or the advertiser telling them so. Your voice can create change.

   Find the name, address, or e-mail address of the magazine's editor/publisher on one of the front pages. You can often locate an advertiser by calling toll-free directory assistance and asking them to look up the name of the company: 1-800-555-1212.

   Your letter can include three sections: (1) a statement of the problem/what you find offensive, (2) a statement of how you feel/what you think about the problem, (3) a statement of what you'd like the magazine/advertiser to do differently. Be sure to include your return address! You may get a response.

Eating: A Questionnaire

Do you (**A**)gree or (**D**)isagree with the following statements? Circle the letter to indicate your choice. If you're not sure, write down the reasons why.

A D   1. Eating makes you smart.

A D   2. I can reshape my body to look like a model's.

A D   3. A lot of diets cause you to gain weight, not lose it.

A D   4. When you're really mad at someone, getting a treat to eat is a good way to make yourself feel better.

A D   5. Eating makes you strong.

A D   6. Vegetables are the most important food to eat each day.

A D   7. Everyone should eat the same size portions at a meal.

A D   8. Fat in foods is bad for you.

A D   9. It's really important to eat three meals a day.

A D   10. Snacking after school is bad for you.

Snack Attack!

Everybody snacks, especially people who may not be able to get all the nutrients they need at a meal. Do you miss out on regular meals because of a busy schedule? Are you active in sports? Do you need more energy during the day? Then try snacking! Choose snacks thoughtfully—power foods, not junk—to keep you healthy and strong.

★ Satisfying Tastes and Textures ★

Sometimes we crave snacks for their textures and how they'll feel and taste in our mouths. Here are some things you may not have already tried…

Finger foods: grapes, strawberries, blueberries, bananas, cherry tomatoes, raisins, dates, almonds, figs, dried pears or apricots, low-fat cheese sticks.

Crunchy snacks: baby carrots, celery sticks, cucumber slices, pepper strips, rice or popcorn cakes, "light" popcorn, whole-grain crackers, breadsticks, flat bread, graham crackers, pretzels, low-fat granola bars, pickles.

Refreshing snacks: fruit salad, melon wedges, oranges, grapefruit, kiwi, pineapple, sorbet, sherbet, Italian ice, frozen fruit popsicles, frozen grapes, vegetable juice, orange juice, apple juice, berry juice, homemade lemonade, herbal iced tea.

Soothing snacks: fruit smoothies, applesauce, pudding, yogurt with added fruit, vegetable soup, chicken soup, bean soup, hot chocolate made with low-fat milk.

★ High-Energy Power Snacks ★

Combine carbohydrates and low-fat protein to satisfy your appetite and give you the best stamina and endurance. Here are some ideas.

low-fat yogurt	whole-grain crackers	flour tortilla
granola	low-fat cheese	peanut butter and raisins
fruit slices	juice	low-fat milk
1 pizza slice	pita bread	fruit smoothie: strawberries, ice, berry
1 cup of juice	turkey, lettuce, tomato	juice, vanilla yogurt, protein powder
flat bread	whole-grain cereal	wholegrain bread
cottage cheese	low-fat milk	tuna
fruit slices	banana	lemonade

What Is Normal Eating?

★ Normal eating is going to the table hungry and **eating until you are satisfied**.

★ Normal eating is **choosing food you like** and eating it and truly getting enough of it—and not just stopping eating because you think you should.

★ Normal eating is **giving some thought** to your food selection so you get nutritious food, but not being so cautious that you miss out on enjoyable food.

★ Normal eating is sometimes **giving yourself permission** to eat because you are happy, sad, bored, or just because eating feels good.

★ Normal eating is **three meals** per day—or four of five smaller meals—(with snacks).

★ Normal eating is **leaving some cookies** on the plate because you know you can have some tomorrow, or it is **eating more now** because they taste so wonderful.

★ Normal eating is **overeating at times**, feeling stuffed and uncomfortable. It is also **undereating at times** and wishing you had more.

★ Normal eating is **trusting your body** to make up for your "mistakes" in eating.

★ Normal eating takes up some of your time and attention, but keeps its place as **only one important area** of your life.

★ Normal eating is **flexible**. It varies in response to your hunger, your schedule, your feelings, and food availability.

If you aren't sure what normal eating means for you, here are some professionals who can help you out (or direct you to the right person who can): your doctor/gynecologist, school nurse, school nutritionist, guidance counselor, health teacher, physical education teacher.

Source: Reprinted and slightly revised from *Secrets of Feeding a Healthy Family* (p. 5) by Ellyn Satter with permission of Kelcy Press, 1999.

Mommy, May I?

Cut the following scenarios into strips and place them in a paper bag.

1. As a mommy, you're responsible for planning and preparing what your daughter eats each day, including food at home and at school. Map out a day's sample menu for your 8-year-old. Include three meals and however many snacks you think are best for her.

2. Your daughter traipses downstairs before school. "Mommy, I don't wanta eat breakfast," she says. "I'm not hungry so early in the morning." What do you say? What do you do?

3. Your daughter always gets hungry halfway through her gymnastics class, but she refuses to eat a snack beforehand, even though she knows she gets hungry later. What do you say? What do you do?

4. "Mommy, let's go to McDonald's!" your daughter shouts in the car. You are in a hurry and pull into the parking lot. She's jumping up and down in her seat with excitement. Once inside, she can't decide what to order and says, "Mommy, you choose for me." What are the most nutritious foods to order?

5. Your daughter's gaining unneeded weight and you think you know why. She goes to her best friend's house each day after school where they snack on junk food all afternoon— foods high in sugar and fat but low in nutrition like candy bars, chips, and ice cream. What do you say? What do you do?

6. You and your daughter and some of her friends go out for ice cream. Your daughter insists, "I'm not getting ice cream. Ice cream makes you fat." Your daughter is at a healthy weight for her age. What do you say?

Call to Action
Unit 6: Nourishing Our Bodies

Action is the test of our success. Let's demonstrate our commitment to ourselves, to one another, and to making a positive difference in the world.

★ Personal Action ★

1. Make mealtime a relaxed and joyful experience.

This week, try to eat at least two meals in the most pleasurable way possible. For example:

- Set a pretty table. Light some candles, put some flowers in the center of the table, put down placemats and napkins.
- Avoid mean or upsetting conversations while eating.
- Eat consciously. Make your focus the sensual pleasures of eating: the smells, tastes, textures, colors of foods. That means no distractions! No radio or TV; no books, magazines, or comics.
- Take a few minutes to consider the many hands it took to get food to your table: the women and men in warm climates who pick the fruits and vegetables, the truckers who drive the produce to market, the cows that supply milk and the farmers who care for them, the grocery store employees who stock the shelves, and so on. Give thanks!

★ Action at Home ★

2. Who plans the menu at home?

Sit down and talk with them about what you've learned about "power" foods (a variety of unprocessed foods, as close as possible to their natural form, bursting with vitamins and minerals). Show them the list of healthy snacks. Then take action!

- Look through the cupboards together to see what's in stock—both power foods and junk foods.
- Talk about some new foods to try.
- Go grocery shopping with a family member and choose a variety of power-packed snacks.

★ Action in the World ★

3. Find a "power" food you really like and bring some to next week's group to share.

4. Be an investigative team!

With a fellow group member, check out the nutritional health of your school. Take notes. Start with the cafeteria: What's being served for lunch this week? Is there variety? Are foods tasty? Healthy? Power-packed? How are foods prepared: steamed, grilled, fried? Does the school offer students an array of powerful snacks? Are there soda and candy machines or fruit juice, milk, and power snack machines?

What could be improved? What do you think needs changing? Write down your findings and suggestions, and be ready to report at next session.

Menu of Hungers: What's Eating You?

We human beings need to get fed every day—in lots of different ways. When we feel "tummy hunger," it's time to eat and rehydrate our bodies. We have other hungers, too—like the need for friends or for alone time—and food doesn't satisfy these. The next time you find yourself reaching for something to eat, stop and ask yourself: What am I *really* hungry for? What would *really* satisfy me?

Read through the menu and see if anything looks appetizing. Check actions that make sense for you. Write down more ideas underneath.

Intellectual Hunger: Needs stimulation

☐ Visit the library
☐ Have a great conversation
☐ Log onto a fascinating website
☐ Watch an interesting movie
☐
☐
☐

Solitude Hunger: Needs space

☐ Take a bath
☐ Walk in the woods
☐ Close the door and lie on the floor
☐ Write in my journal
☐
☐
☐

Spiritual Hunger: Needs meaning

☐ Pray
☐ Sing a song
☐ Read or write a poem
☐ Light a candle and meditate
☐
☐
☐

Physical Hunger: Needs movement

☐ Run
☐ Jump rope
☐ Dance
☐ Play basketball
☐
☐
☐

Friendship Hunger: Needs companionship

☐ Call a friend
☐ Sign up for a club or team
☐ Do a good deed
☐ Consider whether I have the right people in my life
☐
☐

Creative Hunger: Needs invention

☐ Play an instrument
☐ Write a letter
☐ Cook a meal
☐ Build something
☐
☐
☐

Call to Action
Unit 7: Feeding Our Many Appetites

> Action is the test of our success. Let's demonstrate our commitment to ourselves, to one another, and to making a positive difference in the world.

★ Personal Action ★

1. Meditate for 2 minutes every day.

Choose a regular time and place to meditate; for example, right before dinner or right before brushing your teeth in the morning. Use a peaceful image or an inspiring or soothing word for your mantra. You might try a different sentence from the "Full of Ourselves Proclamation" for your focus each day.

2. Write in a journal for at least 10 minutes at the end of each day.

Express yourself however you need.

3. Check in with your many appetites.

Whenever you find yourself reaching for something to eat, stop and ask yourself first: What am I *really* hungry for? What will *really* satisfy me? If your tummy's hungry, eat or drink something delicious! If you're not hungry for food, take time to figure out what kind of nourishment you really need. Do you need to get up and move? To lie down and relax? To connect with a friend? To tackle an assignment you've been avoiding? Refer to the "Menu of Hungers" and see if anything looks appetizing to you.

★ Action at Home ★

4. Interview two adults.

Ask them this question: When you get stressed out, what do you do to make yourself feel better?

Constellation of Connection

━━━━━━━━━━ strong connection

— — — — — — connection not as strong as you'd like

∿∿∿∿∿∿ connection under tension and stress

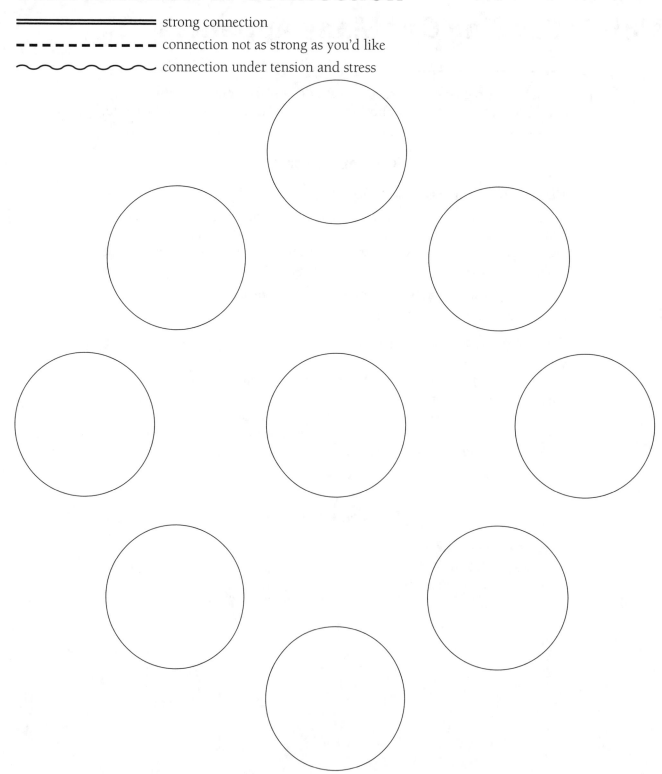

　　　Full of Ourselves, Copyright © 2006 by Teachers College, Columbia University

Conflict Case Studies

★ Case 1 ★

One of your closest friends comes running up to you with big news. She's going to sneak out this weekend, go downtown, and meet an older boy she hardly knows. She's so excited. You are the only one she's told, and she asks you to keep this a secret. Your heart sinks. You feel scared for her, and in your gut you know this is all wrong. But you can see in her face how much she wants you to be happy for her. She asks your advice about what to wear. What do you say or do?

★ Case 2 ★

It's Sunday afternoon and you've got your whole day planned out: when you're going to do your homework, when you're going to talk to your boyfriend, and when you're going to meet your friends. In the middle of your homework, your mom comes to your room and tells you that you have to babysit. You can't believe it! It's already three o'clock, and you can't believe she's just telling you now. This completely messes up the rest of your plans. You're furious! What do you say or do?

★ Case 3 ★

You and Samantha have a tentative date to go to the mall together on Saturday. But then you hear from Heather that she and Samantha are going to the mall to-gether—*without you*. It's clear that you're being left out. What do you say or do?

★ Case 4 ★

You are standing by your locker talking with two good friends when one of them says, "I can't believe I wore these jeans! My thighs look so *fat*!" "What are you talk-ing about?" the other girl says, "*I'm* the one who's fat." You look at your friends. Who are they kidding? They are both tall, thin girls who, in fact, probably wear the same size. You know that they are expecting you to bad-mouth your body, too. But you're tired of doing this. It's phony, it's meaningless, and it makes everybody feel bad. What do you say or do?

★ Case 5 ★

You're at a party and everyone starts pairing off to slow-dance and make out. You're one of the few girls left without a partner, and you're feeling really awkward. A boy you don't like very much comes up and asks you to dance. You agree—it sure beats standing all alone—but in the middle of the dance he moves to start kissing you. What do you say or do?

Call to Action Contract

★ I promise to try to combat weightism in myself and in my community.

★ I promise to try to understand, respect, and include other people, no matter what they look like.

★ I promise to try to honor and accept myself, just the way I am.

★ I will do my best to eat healthfully and to nourish all of my many appetites.

★ I will try to make the world a better place by being "full of myself" in the best sense of the phrase and by "throwing my weight around" in healthy ways.

Signature _____

Date _____

Witnesses _____

_____

_____

_____

_____

_____

_____

_____

_____

We're in this together, differences included!

Full of Ourselves, *Copyright © 2006 by Teachers College, Columbia University*

Yoga Primer

Introduction to Yoga Practice
(Time Estimate: 5–10 minutes)

⟳ Pose the following question and draw from the sample script, as needed: "Have any of you ever practiced yoga? Can someone describe what yoga is?"

❝ Yoga is the general term for a broad field of study that began in India about 5,000 years ago. At its most basic, yoga is a type of exercise that builds physical strength, flexibility, and coordination. But yoga is much more than just physical exercise: It builds strength and flexibility of mind as well as body. Yoga develops greater mental clarity, focus, and concentration—qualities essential for success in all areas of your life.

'Yoga' literally means 'to join.' The purpose of yoga is to bring your physical and mental energies into synch, to develop a healthy body and a sound mind at the same time. In this culture, we tend to divide body and mind into separate entities. Yoga is about interconnectedness.

Yoga requires that you take up space, literally and metaphorically. It also increases your awareness; it helps you get in touch with yourself and your place in the world."

⟳ Review these three helpful reminders:

1. *Loose clothing is best for yoga.* If needed, untuck your shirt and release the top buttons or zipper on your pants so you can move and breathe more freely.
2. *Never strain.* We work best when we are relaxed, and all movements in yoga are to be as slow and easy as possible. Breathing will help you to move with ease.
3. *Yoga is not competitive.* Each of you should work at your own pace and try to stay aware of your own limits. When you try to force a posture, you wind up discouraging your body.

⟳ Pose a warm-up question:

❝ How would you describe yourself and your energy today? Do you feel airy, light, maybe even spacey? Or heavy and lethargic?
Wherever you are energetically, doing yoga postures will help you find more inner balance."

Energetic Warm-Up: Arm Swing

⟳ *Starting Points:* We're going to do a breathing exercise to get oxygen flowing through our veins and rev up our circulation. Think of your breath as coming from your belly, not from your throat. Your belly is your energy center, and the life force in the body comes from the air you breathe.

Arm Swing:
1. Everyone find your own space with enough room to move freely. Stand straight with your feet a few inches apart.
2. Now begin to swing your arms from side to side.

3. As you swing them faster and they wrap fully around each side of your body, say the word "Hah" on each out-breath. As in the martial arts, yoga uses the breath and voice to access inner power and strength.

Energetic Warm-Up: Wood Chopper

⊃ *Starting Points:* Life force comes from the air you breathe. The more oxygen you take into your lungs, the more energetic and alive you feel. The goal of this warm-up is to rev up our circulation by increasing the flow of oxygen through our bodies. Let your breath come from your belly, not your throat. Your belly is your energy center.

Woodchopper:

1. Stand straight with your feet a shoulder-width apart and planted firmly on the ground. Feel yourself well balanced, not too rigid and not too limp.
2. Raise your arms straight overhead, palms resting lightly together, and take in a deep breath.
3. On an exhale, swing your arms down and between your legs.
4. Swing back up again overhead and down in a fluid motion, inhaling and exhaling, as though you were swinging an axe to chop wood. Your knees will bend as you do this.
5. On each out-breath, say the word "Hah!" Sometimes it can feel a little embarrassing to make noise together, but it's a really important part of the warm-up that helps us access our inner power.
6. Try this 10 times.

Mountain Pose

⊃ *Starting Points:* We can look at every yoga posture symbolically. Yoga poses are named for the kind of energy they embody. What do you think of when you think of a mountain?

❝ Mountains are very stable and solid. They last a long time. They have a wide base and are solid on the ground. They also peak toward the sky. In a mountain, the energy of the earth is wedded with the energy of the sky."

Mountain Pose:

1. Stand with your feet parallel and a hip-width apart. Shift your weight to the balls of your feet and press the soles of your feet downward. Feel yourself connected to the energy of the earth.
2. Keep your knees strong, but not locked. Locking your knees blocks the flow of energy.
3. Press the crown of your head gently away from your shoulders, with your chin tucked slightly in and down, and feel how this slight movement elongates your spine. Make sure your shoulders aren't hunched up near your ears.
4. Are you breathing? Take a few slow breaths from your belly.
5. Allow your fingertips to rise overhead and turn your palms to face each other. They should be about a shoulder-width apart.
6. Remember to keep breathing! Allow your chest to expand.
7. Don't stand too rigidly in place—but also don't be too limp. Try to find a comfortable balance as you breathe.
8. It might seem like you are simply standing. But you are standing with great awareness and intention. Notice your feet rooted to the ground. Notice your arms searching the sky. You are in *mountain* pose.
9. On an exhale, slowly lower your arms down to your sides. Inhale and raise them up

Mountain Pose

again—as though you were in slow motion. Try this simple movement a few times, co-ordinating with your breath.

10. Now let's try an experiment: Let your arms hang down, all floppy. Let your shoulders slump. How does this feel? Does this look like a mountain to you?

11. Now regain mountain pose and straighten your arms to the sky once again, with your shoulders down, not up near your ears. You are creating a smooth, long passage-way for life energy and inner power to flow through you. We are tapping into power with intention.

⤴ *Post-pose Conversation:* How does poor posture affect your breathing?

" Your lungs and heart have to work harder if you close up the front of your body. Yoga encourages you to stand and sit with an open posture and let the power of breath move freely through you."

(Peaceful) Warrior Poses

⤴ *Starting Points:* Remember that we can look at yoga practice—and every yoga posture—symboli-cally. Yoga poses are named for the kind of energy they embody. When you think of a warrior, what words come to mind?

" The two warrior poses are about power, but not about violence or aggression. These poses help you connect to your own inner power and cour-age. They concern courage, strength, standing on your feet, being grounded in the world. Think of yourself as a peaceful warrior: someone who is indeed very powerful but who uses her power to create, rather than to hurt or destroy. You can be a warrior in spirit to overcome obstacles and be successful in any situation. If one day you have to say or do something hard, try doing a warrior pose beforehand to tap into courage and power."

Warrior 1 Pose:

1. Stand facing forward with your feet wide apart, about the length of one of your legs.
2. Turn your right foot straight out toward the right and *angle* the toes of the left foot

in toward the right as well (at about 60 degrees).

3. Tuck your bottom under (slight pelvic tilt).
4. Press the crown of your head away from your shoulders, with your chin tucked slightly down. Feel how this movement elongates your spine.
5. Turn your bellybutton and torso to the right to face your leading leg.
6. Raise your arms overhead, palms facing one another, and press your fingertips up to-ward the sky. Make sure to keep your shoul-ders down, instead of hunched up toward your ears.
7. Breathe!
8. Bend your right knee and sink into the posture. Your knee should be lined up with your ankle.
9. Keep much of your weight on your *back* leg. Your upper body should be perpendicular to the ground, not leaning forward.
10. Press your back heel downward and feel the stretch in the back of your leg.
11. Remember to keep breathing! Expand your chest by gently pressing it out.
12. Hold the posture for 10–20 seconds—or for as long as you can. Notice how this requires strength, balance, and concentration.
13. To release, exhale and bring your arms to your sides, and then straighten your right leg. Turn your torso and feet to the center. Take a deep breath.

Warrior 1 Pose

Warrior 2 Pose:

1. Stand with your feet wide apart, about the length of one of your legs.
2. Turn the toes of your right foot directly out to the right side.
3. Angle the left foot in toward the right as well.
4. Gently tuck your bottom under (a slight pelvic tilt).
5. Press the crown of your head away from your shoulders, with your chin tucked slightly down and in. Feel how this little movement elongates your spine.
6. Extend your arms and fingertips out to your sides at shoulder level and press gently away from your shoulders.
7. *Note:* keep your bellybutton facing directly ahead. Unlike Warrior 1, don't turn your torso to face over your right leg.
8. Bend your right knee and sink into the posture. Your knee should be lined up above your ankle.
9. Your upper body should be straight, not leaning forward.
10. Remember to keep breathing!
11. Turn your head to gaze out toward the fingertips of your right hand.
12. Hold the posture for 10–20 seconds, while breathing. Inhale as you straighten your spine, and exhale as you reach out through your fingertips. Notice how this requires strength, balance, and concentration.

13. To release, straighten your right leg, exhale, and bring your arms down to your sides and your feet forward.

⊃ Repeat on the opposite side. Don't skip this step! It helps keep the body balanced.

Child Pose

⊃ *Starting Points:* What words come to mind when you think of a tiny sleeping baby?

" Child pose is a nurturing pose, a 'cool' pose meant to help calm down your energy as you assume a natural fetal position. Try doing this pose when you are vulnerable or upset; it will help to give you a sense of safety, as all of your vulnerable inner organs are protected."

Child Pose:

1. Sit on your heels and press your tailbone downward.
2. Gently press the crown of your head upward, away from your shoulders.
3. Lift your tailbone and allow your torso to come forward with your forehead resting on the floor and your arms draped back by your sides.
4. You can also try resting your forehead on the backs of your hands. Or you can let your hands rest, palms down, on the floor next to your head.
5. Relax into the pose and be aware of your calming breath.
6. Rest in pose for 20 seconds or longer.

Child Pose

Warrior 2 Pose

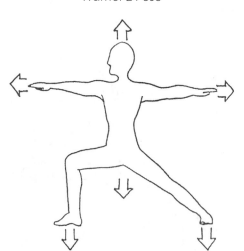

Deep Relaxation/Corpse Pose

⊃ *Starting Point:*

" Yoga consists of a lot of physical motion. It is also important to allow your body to just 'be' and to still and quiet your mind, free from all distraction. Deep relaxation allows you to cope more easily with both physical and mental stress. It also allows you to regain the energy you have just used in the yoga postures and to feel refreshed and renewed."

Corpse Pose:

1. Lie on your back with your eyes closed.
2. Allow your legs to relax, with your heels slightly apart. Allow your heels to fall outward.
3. Lower your shoulders and let your arms rest comfortably at your sides, slightly away from your body. Allow your palms to open toward the sky like a flower's petals. Imagine warm sunlight in the hollow of your hands.
4. Now rock your head gently from side to side until it finds a comfortable position. Tip your chin slightly to your chest.
5. Notice the rise and fall of your body as you breathe in and out. Each time you exhale, allow yourself to sink more deeply into the floor.
6. Bring your attention to your legs and let them feel light (pause)
7. Bring your attention to your lower body and let it feel light (pause)
8. Now relax your upper body and let it feel light (pause)
9. Relax your arms and let them feel light (pause)
10. Relax your jaw and your mouth . . . your eyes and your ears . . . the muscles of your scalp . . .
11. Imagine that a quilt is covering you up to your neck. You are warm and very relaxed.
12. Now imagine you are a light, fluffy cloud, floating in a beautiful blue sky. Let any thoughts drift through your mind like a soft breeze and gently bring your attention back to your breathing.

13. Allow at least 2 full minutes of quiet relaxation

Coming Out of Corpse Pose:

1. Begin to deepen your breath.
2. Wiggle your fingers and your toes.
3. Stretch your arms and your legs in any way that feels comfortable to you.
4. Hug your knees to your chest and gently rock from side to side.
5. When you feel ready, roll completely over to one side and bring yourself up to sitting.
6. Stretch your body in any way that feels good to you.
7. You are alert and refreshed, ready for work or play.

Final Debriefing

⊃ Pose the following questions to debrief:

1. Compare your energy now to when you started. Notice any differences?
2. Recall how you felt in each of these yoga postures. Did you feel comfortable in the warrior poses? In the child pose?
3. Did one pose feel more natural to you than another?

" Some people may naturally be in 'warrior' mode more often, and they could use more child energy in their lives. Other people may operate more often in 'child' mode, and they need to tap more warrior energy to achieve inner balance—physically and mentally."

Disordered Eating and Eating Disorders—Background Information

Anorexia nervosa. Bulimia nervosa. Binge-eating disorder. These three terms are notably absent from the curriculum. Because our aim is prevention, we purposefully avoid mention of these diseases. This is *not* a curriculum to teach girls what eating disorders are or to scare girls out of getting one. Study after study has found that discussions about specific disordered eating "practices" actually do more harm than good (e.g., confessional-style talks by former anorexics or bulimics). Girls get potentially harmful ideas and, rather than being scared off, a percentage of girls think instead: "She got through an eating disorder and look how great she looks. Maybe I'll start dieting/purging/using laxatives for a while, just until I lose some weight; then I'll stop."

We caution you against discussing particular eating disorders or warning signs with girls. Instead, approach each session with the clear intention of *advancing girl power, health, and leadership*. We believe that eating disorders are a culturally mediated and culturally supported set of behaviors that girls adopt when life gets too stressful, overwhelming, or hard. Therefore, these units aim to give girls a chance to learn and practice alternative ways of responding to stress.

That being said, here is some background information to help you to understand just what this program aims to prevent.

Disordered Eating

Disordered eating refers to mild or transient changes in eating patterns that occur in relation to a stressful event, an illness, or a desire to change one's diet for athletic, health, or personal appearance reasons. Disordered eating can be a bad habit or a style of eating adopted from friends or family members. While disordered eating can lead to weight loss, weight gain, or nutritional problems, it rarely requires in-depth professional attention. Even so, disordered eating, especially extreme dieting, is a frequent precursor of the later development of eating disorders. Research suggests that 13% of teenage girls, though not yet diagnosed with full-blown eating disorders, engage in disordered anorexic and bulimic *behaviors* such as self-induced vomiting, laxative and diet pill abuse, skipping meals, and cycles of binge-eating and dieting.

Dieting

Dieting for weight loss, a common precursor of eating disorders, is extremely common among teenage girls. Fifty percent of 10-year-old girls say they are afraid of being fat, just at the developmental moment where menarche necessitates added weight gain. Nearly 50% of girls in high school think they are overweight—and diet.

Obesity

Obesity is on the rise among American girls. Along with numerous serious health consequences, obesity can influence girls' social and economic potential in a culture that values thinness in females. Ironically, dieting contributes to the rising rates of obesity; "fad" dieting routinely results in unhealthy eating, particularly bingeing and consumption of high-fat junk foods.

Eating Disorders

In contrast to disordered eating, eating disorders are not mere bad habits. They are illnesses that usually do not go away without specific medical attention. Eating disorders typically refer to anorexia nervosa, bulimia nervosa, or binge-eating disorder. Generally, they are distinct syndromes, but individuals can suffer from a combination of conditions. The common notion persists that only middle- and upper-middle-class White girls develop disordered eating and eating disorders. This is a misperception: Research indicates that girls from African American, Asian, Native American, and Hispanic families, as well as girls from every class background, are all affected by eating disorders and disturbances.

Anorexia Nervosa

Anorexia commonly begins in a teenager who is overweight or perceives herself to be so. What often starts as an effort to lose weight escalates into an obsession with thinness and a profound deterioration in eating habits. Girls with anorexia try to control their weight by radically restricting food intake, purging calories through vomiting or use of laxatives, and exercising compulsively. Medical complications of chronic anorexia can include osteoporosis, a thinning of the bones that can lead to fractures and vertebral collapse, and electrolyte abnormalities that can provoke potentially fatal heart-rhythm disturbances.

Bulimia Nervosa

Young women with bulimia may be of normal weight or overweight. The disorder is characterized by secretive episodes of binge-eating huge amounts of food followed by some form of purging: self-induced vomiting, fasting, the use of laxatives or diuretics, or overexercising. Major medical complications of bulimia include gastrointestinal problems and electrolyte abnormalities.

Binge-Eating Disorder

Binge-eating is a normal behavior for many people, particularly during times of stress, during transitions, or on special occasions. When binge-eating begins to occur more often—at least twice a week for a 6-month period—a girl may be struggling with a more serious problem. Binge-eating is characterized by the consumption of a large quantity of food in a relatively short (e.g., 2-hour) period of time, coupled with the sense of being out of control and not being able to stop eating. These episodes usually involve eating more rapidly than usual and until uncomfortably full. Possible complications include unhealthful weight gain, weight-related hypertension, diabetes, and high blood pressure.

Prevalence of Disordered Eating

Dieting and disordered eating, often considered "normal" behaviors in girls, are not benign developmental rites of passage; they have serious negative physiological, psychological, and behavioral affects. In practical terms: It is not unusual for a 14-year-old girl to think that she will be in better control of and happier with her life—evidenced by more friends, closer ties with teachers, higher grades, and more celebrated accomplishments—if she skips lunch. The bigger picture: Full-blown eating disorders are now the third most common chronic illness among females, and their prevalence among teens and preteen girls is growing.

Warning Signs for Eating Disorders

Eating disorders are serious illnesses; the longer the symptoms persist, the harder it is to successfully treat the disorder. The sooner warning signs and symptoms are recognized and responded to, the better the prognosis. That said, because many people are concerned with weight and diet at least occasionally, it can be difficult to tell what is normal behavior and what is a problem that may escalate to an eating disorder. Below is a list of warning signs to help you identify the presence of an eating disorder. While it is rare for one person to display all of these warning signs, people with eating disorders often manifest several of them.

1. Excessive preoccupation with weight/weighing, food, calories, and/or dieting
2. Excessive and/or compulsive exercise regimen: the need to "burn off" calories regardless of bad weather, fatigue, sickness, and/or injury

3. Withdrawal from activities because of the presence of food and/or weight and shape concerns
4. Evidence of self-induced vomiting or use of laxatives, diuretics, purgatives, enemas, or diet pills
5. Evidence of binge-eating, including hoarding and/or stealing food
6. Alternating periods of severely restricting dieting and overeating, often accompanied by dramatic weight fluctuations
7. Other unusual eating behaviors: skipping meals, eating tiny portions, fear of eating in front of other people, ritualistic or secretive eating, cooking for others but not participating in eating/enjoying the food
8. Abnormal weight loss of 25% or more, with no known medical illness accounting for the loss
9. Distorted body image and/or anxiety about being fat/weight gain/obesity that does not diminish as weight is lost
10. Loss or irregularity of the menstrual cycle or inexplicable problems with menstruation (in females)

10 Tips for Parents—How Best to Support Full of Ourselves at Home

Remember: There's no such thing as a "joke" about someone's body. Research shows that teasing and harassment contribute to the development of eating disorders.

Set a good example through your own actions. Do not go on any "fad" or magazine diets. These don't work! In the long run, they lead to weight gain, not loss. If you need help with your own relationship to food, see a nutritionist, doctor, or counselor and let your daughter know that you are on a medically supervised diet and that your goal is to eat healthfully and create a healthier lifestyle. Let her know that you take yourself and your health seriously.

The same goes for words! Never put yourself down for how you look in front of your daughter. Don't tolerate anyone else putting you—or your daughter or another person—down for how you look. And try not to greet friends with comments about how they look. Instead, practice taking people seriously for what they think, say, and do, not for how slender, "buff," or well put together they are.

Do not subscribe to the "morality of orality." Avoid labeling particular foods or your own eating habits as "good" or "bad"; for example, "I was so *bad* today—I ate a hot fudge sundae."

Wear clothes that express who you are, regardless of your size or shape. Don't let your body shape keep you from doing things you want simply because you don't "look the part."

Keep an eye out for weightist messages in the media with your daughter. Name, discuss, and refute them! The point is not to deny that weightism exists or to pretend that weightist comments aren't painful. Instead, help your daughter draw useful parallels between weightism and other forms of prejudice: Remind her that judging someone solely on the basis of their body size or shape can be as cruel as judging them solely on the basis of their skin color, sex, or religion. Reassure her that there are many ways we can together learn to fight weightism in the world and inside ourselves.

Take stock of your cupboards! Are they filled with foods from all food groups? What kinds of snacks do you keep on hand? Supply your kitchen with a variety of low-cost, high-health foods.

Avoid using food as a reward or punishment. Find ways other than shopping or eating to celebrate your small victories on any given day. Likewise, when your daughter is upset, try going for a walk and talking together—rather than going out to eat. Or make her a cup of tea, sit down with her, and let her know you are *really* there for her. Your time is one of the most nourishing resources you can offer her.

Let your daughter know that you love her, no matter what she weighs! Listen to her opinions, show appreciation for her uniqueness, and, as often as possible, allow her to take the lead. If you are worried about her weight, talk to her pediatrician or a nutritionist.

★ Take stock of your own body image and attitudes. In a journal, or with a friend or spouse, consider the following questions. There are no right or wrong answers. We all begin in different places in terms of body acceptance and awareness.

- How did I develop my own body image? What was I told about my body and appearance when I was young?

- How accepting or rejecting am I of my body shape and size? How often are my comments to myself about how I look positive? How often negative?

- What are my attitudes toward people of differing body sizes and shapes? How do I express these attitudes? Do I ever feel better or worse about myself because I think my body is superior or inferior to theirs?

- Have I or has someone I know ever been discriminated against or hurt by comments made about body shape or size? How have I responded?

- What degree of emphasis do I put on my daughter's body size and shape? Do I ever relay the message that I will like her more if she looks different?

Sample Letters to Parents

Letter 1: Program Announcement and Description

Dear 7th-Grade Parents,

We are writing to tell you about an exciting new educational project for girls called Full of Ourselves: Advancing Girl Power, Health, and Leadership and to welcome your daughter's participation. Developed by professionals at the Harvard Medical School, Full of Ourselves is a program for healthy, growing girls in middle schools across the country. The goal of the program is to help girls stay healthy and confident by teaching them healthy attitudes and behaviors about eating, exercise, and body image.

This [15-week] program will begin in [month, year]. The program is divided into two parts. During the first part, girls explore a variety of topics: self and body acceptance, media literacy and ways to counter unhealthy media messages, how to respond to teasing and bullying based on weight, techniques for dealing with stress, nutrition basics, the power of positive thinking and action, and the importance of healthy relationships. During the second part, girls will get a chance to develop leadership skills by designing, and then leading, activities for younger girls.

The sessions will be led by [names and credentials of site leaders]. The sessions will be held on [day of week] from [time] beginning on [start date] and will continue through [end date].

Your daughter has expressed an interest in participating in this upbeat program with [number of girls in group] other 7th-grade girls. Our hope is that, by the end of the sessions, she'll feel more confident, be more accepting of herself and her body, and be less vulnerable to the development of disordered eating. It is our expectation that she'll have lots of fun and maybe make some new friends, too! If you agree to her participate in the group, please fill out the attached permission form and have your daughter return it to [name of adult in charge of collecting forms] by [deadline].

We are sponsoring a Parent Information Night on [date] to tell you more about the goals and philosophy of this exciting program. Please come, try on some program activities for size, and learn how to support the program at home.

We are looking forward to working with your daughter and thank you in advance for your interest and support.

Sincerely,

Letter 2: Program Update

Dear Parents,

Your daughter attended her first Full of Ourselves session this week. The group is off to a good start; the girls clearly enjoy each other and are enthusiastic about participating in the program. Already we are struck by their intelligence, candor, and sense of humor. We feel privileged to hear their thoughts.

Your daughter will attend FOO sessions [every Tuesday after school from 3:15–4:30 from now until the end of the school year]. We will meet [in the art room].

During the first few months of the program, the girls will explore a variety of topics related to health, nutrition, media literacy, and "weightism" (a form of prejudice based on body size and shape). The group will be involved in discussions, role plays, skits, games, and journal writing. During [month], the girls will become "girl leaders" and design and lead a few sessions with younger girls. We are in the process of finding a group of younger girls (ages 8–10) who would be eager to work with us. If you have a younger daughter or if you know of a group (Brownies, etc.) that might be interested, please let us know.

We are excited to be working with your daughter and are confident that the sessions will be filled with lively, meaningful learning. Please don't hesitate to contact us if you have any concerns.

Best wishes,

10 Tips for Schools—Create a Culture that Supports Student Well-Being

As you set out to implement Full of Ourselves with girls, create a school-wide setting that supports this eating disorders prevention/health promotion initiative. Here are 10 places to start.

1. Get as many staff members on board as possible.

Request time at a faculty meeting to present the major program themes. Encourage faculty to model acceptance of diverse body shapes, sizes, and appearances—starting with their own. Create a protocol of acceptable topics of discussion; for instance, it is not appropriate for teachers to comment on one another's or a student's weight, no matter how well-intentioned. Provide professional development on health, nutrition, and the signs and symptoms of eating disorders.

2. Provide a range of affordable, fresh, nutritious foods.

Work with food service to ensure greater consistency between food choices in the cafeteria and nutrition information taught in Health class. Eliminate vending machines—or stock them with healthier choices.

3. Check out the visual images in your school.

Do they promote well-being and acceptance of body size diversity? For example, do the posters, books, magazines, videos, and artwork displayed in the school reflect a range of body shapes and appearances?

4. Don't weigh kids publicly—ever.

Don't weigh kids on the first day of school. Avoid placing scales in public places (such as locker rooms) where students with body and/or weight preoccupation can ruin their ability to concentrate by getting on the scale.

5. Review your school's anti-harassment and anti-discrimination policies.

Do these include injustices based on physical appearance and body size or shape? Provide students with both formal and informal avenues to report in-cidents of teasing, bullying, or harassment. Include information on weightism in all school diversity awareness campaigns.

6. Don't discriminate or play favorites on the basis of appearance.

In particular, watch out for favoritism of girls who fit the cultural definition of "pretty." Whenever possible, see that students of diverse body sizes are chosen as leaders for a variety of tasks (i.e., as school representatives, in theatrical productions, as team captains, etc.).

7. Educate parents.

Host an evening forum to inform all interested parents and other relatives about the content of Full of Ourselves and how to prevent eating disorders at home.

8. Designate a school eating disorders resource team.

This might include a school nurse, counselor, teacher, and other staff members who are interested in enhancing students' health. Provide training about eating disorders and treatment. Develop a database of local counseling centers and medical practitioners that serve students with eating disorders and body image issues.

9. Establish policies and protocols that relate specifically to eating disorders.

Create a standard protocol for approaching and referring students with possible eating problems, as well as guidelines for contacting parents and liaising with outside health professionals.

10. Refer at-risk students.

If you are concerned about a student, share your concerns with the eating disorders resource team or other staff members who know the student. Decide together on the best course of action—which may include referral to a qualified professional.

Part Two

Throw Your Weight Around!

Throw Your Weight Around!
A Guide for Adult Leaders

❀ CONTENTS ❀

Program Rationale

During this second program phase, older girls who have completed the Full of Ourselves sessions design and teach activities to younger girls. Assuming the role of peer mentors, older girls have the opportunity to "walk the talk" and apply some of the concepts they learned during the earlier sessions.

Younger girls are less likely to discredit information when it comes from an older girl rather than from a parent, teacher, or other adult authority. Ideally, when the younger girls reach the 7th or 8th grade, they will have the opportunity to participate in the Full of Ourselves sessions and become peer leaders themselves.

The Role of Adult Leaders

Think of yourself as a coach and trainer of a team of young teachers; you need to ensure that the experience is safe, fair, and fun for all involved. Your two main responsibilities are (1) to arrange the sessions with the younger girls and (2) to assist the older girls with lesson planning.

Getting Started

Cover the following steps *before* meeting with your group of older girls.

1. Familiarize yourself with this guide and the *Guide for Girl Leaders*.
2. Photocopy the *Guide for Girl Leaders*, one per older girl.
3. Identify and contact a group of younger girls to partner with the older girls through schools, religious organizations, Brownies, extended-day/after-school programs, and so on. Let the adult in charge know basically what the older girls plan on doing.
4. Send a letter home to the parents of the younger girls explaining phase 2 of the program. Use or revise the sample letter provided at the end of this section.
5. Work out logistics: a meeting place, dates, times, and transportation. Schedule these arrangements as soon as possible.
6. If possible, arrange to have the older girls meet with the younger group casually before they plan their sessions so they can get an idea of whom they will be working with.
7. Get a copy of the storybook *Stephanie's Ponytail* by Robert Munsch (New York: Annick Press, 1996) to read with the older girls at your phase 2 introductory meeting.

Girls' Guide Review

Schedule one meeting with the older girls solely for the purpose of reviewing the *Guide for Girl Leaders*. Sample agenda:

1. Review program goals. Emphasize the important role older girls can play in the lives of younger girls.
2. Read the storybook *Stephanie's Ponytail* together as a group. This is a fun story about an independent girl who refuses to go along with the crowd—and refuses to let a crowd go along with her! Discuss the book in terms of the program title *Throw Your Weight Around*. Do the older girls think this is a good book to read to the younger girls?
3. Discuss what it means to be a girl leader and role model.
4. Review the introductory section of the *Guide for Girl Leaders*. Ask the girls to read aloud the 10 key ideas from Full of Ourselves. Which points interest them the most? What do they wish they'd been told by older girls when they were younger? Examples given by prior participants: puberty facts, how to put on a bra, what to expect with your period, understanding the wide range of "normal," and how to stand up for yourself.
5. Determine how many sessions will transpire with the younger girls. Aim for at least two.
6. Establish ground rules for girl leaders.

Session Planning Meeting(s)

Schedule at least *two* meetings to plan and prepare for each Throw Your Weight Around session with younger girls. Middle school girls are not teachers, so you will need to help them get organized and design a structure in which they are most likely to succeed. For instance, help them be realistic about the number of activities they can complete in a given session with the younger girls. Here are a few more tips to assist with session planning:

1. Encourage the older girls to use the Session Planning Sheets at the back of their guides.
2. Begin by compiling a list of the girls' favorite activities from the Full of Ourselves sessions.
3. Remind the girls that they'll need to "break the ice" and explain ground rules to the younger girls. How would they like to introduce themselves and the program? Encourage them to write out a "Why We're Here" script on note cards.
4. Be sure that responsibilities are shared equitably among the older girls. Be prepared to help the girls with any needed photocopying and supply gathering.
5. Suggest who might make the best "station pairs," especially if any of the pairings seem mismatched in terms of girls' strengths, know-how, and so on.
6. Once the girls design a session, ask them to consider whether it contains anything potentially confusing or upsetting for younger girls. How might they modify these sections?

Stations

Experience suggests that "stations" are the most effective group configuration to adopt in the sessions with the younger girls. Consider the case where the Throw Your Weight Around session with younger girls is 1 hour long:

- Girl leaders divide into three groups, each designated by a certain code name or color (worn on a nametag).
- Each group designs, rehearses, and prepares *one* 15-minute activity to teach the younger girls.
- Younger girls likewise divide into three groups. They can be arbitrarily assigned to groups by color code beforehand. Place a (yellow/red/blue) dot on their nametags.
- Every 15 minutes, the groups of younger girls rotate to different stations. Hence, each group of older girls will teach the same activity three times to three different groups of younger girls.
- The remaining 15 minutes can be used for introductions, an ice-breaker, and a debriefing activity.

> " One of the girls really 'came alive' as she led her station. You could tell she enjoyed the attention, the control, and the interaction with the young girls. What a benefit this program has been for her."
>
> —Adult leader, Massachusetts

Rehearsal Time

Set aside time to rehearse. Share teaching and facilitation tips you and your co-leader used during the Full of Ourselves units. Touch upon the following points, also included on a handout in the *Guide for Girl Leaders:*

1. *Pose lots of questions to get the girls talking.* Respond to an answer with another probing question: "How come? Why do you think that? Will you tell me more about that? Does anyone have a different answer?"
2. *Arrive on time.* If you are 7 minutes late, you may walk into a chaotic room—and there goes your good impression, along with a good chunk of the lesson!
3. *Your body language speaks volumes.* Don't move too far away from the younger girls, and try not to turn your back on anyone.
4. *Make eye contact and smile* to help the younger girls to feel welcome and at ease.
5. *Expect the unexpected.* The more fun an activity, the more excitement! And the more the younger girls will want to talk. Or they may want to take the activity in a whole new direction. It's in these moments that group "magic" can occur. So as you map out your session, don't schedule time too tightly. Allow time for spontaneity.
6. *Be on the lookout for anyone who isn't participating* and invite her into the discussion. "You're not saying much. I'd love to know what you think about _____."
7. *Think of each class as an experiment!* At the end of each class ask yourself what went well, and why, and what you might do differently next time.
8. *Ask for help if you need it.* Give your adult

leaders a high sign if anything goes wrong, if you feel stuck, or if you start to feel shaky.

Throw Your Weight Around! Sessions

Your role is akin to that of a coach: Help your teaching team play fair, follow their game plan, maintain enthusiasm, and have a successful experience. Are the girls prepared? Have they written out an introductory script? Do they have all the needed supplies?

If a teaching situation isn't going well—time or behavior get out of control, a girl leader flounders—lend a hand, but resist the impulse to jump in and override an older girl's authority. Model respect as you would toward any other colleague. For instance, ask permission of the girl leader if you would like to clarify a point or assignment. Or discreetly pull aside one of the girl leaders to make a constructive suggestion. Talk with the older girls *beforehand* about what role(s) they would like adult leaders to play during the sessions.

There is one circumstance when you should definitely intervene: If a younger child says something that older girls don't know how to handle or that indicates she's at risk in any way. In this case, step in immediately and tell the younger girl you will talk with her later. Handle this circumstance as you would any form of disclosure that indicates a child is in danger: Go to the appropriate authority, contact parents, and so on.

Prized Advice from Past Leaders

1. Plan ahead! And make sure the older girls have lots of time to plan and then rehearse.
2. The girls *loved* this! What was difficult, however, was trying to keep myself from controlling everything. During planning sessions, I nudged less active girls into concrete roles and duties. During actual sessions, I made quiet suggestions to the leaders for better interactions between the older and younger girls.
3. Guide the girls toward more active projects with the younger girls.
4. Stay in close contact with the elementary school teacher and principal to make sure everyone's on the same page.
5. Bring a camera to the last session. It's nice to have some formal closure with a group photo session.

Sample Letter for Parents of Younger Girls

(Personalize: Supply meeting dates and times, and describe your work with the older girls and their ideas for phase 2.)

Dear Parent or Guardian:

We are writing to tell you about an exciting new educational project for girls called *Full of Ourselves: A Wellness Program to Advance Girl Power, Health, and Leadership* and to welcome your daughter's participation.

Developed by professionals at the Harvard Medical School, Full of Ourselves is a program for healthy, growing girls in elementary and middle schools across the country. The goal of the program is help girls stay healthy and confident by teaching them healthy attitudes and behaviors about eating, exercise, and body image.

The program has two distinct parts, both upbeat and positive, with emphasis placed on girls' overall mental and physical well-being. Phase 1 involves [6th-, 7th-, 8th-] grade girls and is currently underway at _____. The girls are learning how to spot and combat bullying based on body size and shape. They have looked closely at magazines and other media for messages about bodies, beauty, and health. They have dispelled many myths about dieting and have done some healthy menu planning. They continue to impress us with their openness and astute observations. Our sessions have been marked by boundless energy, companionship, and humor.

During phase 2, the project's leadership component, these same girls will design and lead sessions with [3rd-, 4th-, 5th-] grade girls. They'll work with a curriculum guide to plan activities for the younger girls, and we will supervise the planning and the actual sessions to ensure that activities with the younger girls are safe, educational, age-appropriate, and fun.

It is our expectation that your daughter will benefit and have a great time participating in sessions led by the "big" girls. If you have any questions, give _____ a call at _____ .

Sincerely,

Throw Your Weight Around!
A Guide for Girl Leaders

❧ CONTENTS ❧

INTRODUCTION

Your Mission, Should You Accept It

Throw your weight around with younger girls! You know tons about how to be healthy and confident in the world, how to stand up to meanness and weightism, why fad diets don't work, the importance of eating breakfast, how to do a body scan, ways to take care of yourself when you're upset, and so much more. Now it's time to hand down some of this valuable knowledge to younger girls.

You're the Expert!

And you can make a difference in the lives of younger girls. Because you're older, young girls think you're the greatest. They pay attention to everything you say and do: your words, your attitude, and how well you work together with your friends. Be smart. Exude confidence. Make a positive difference. Most importantly, have fun!

Getting Started

Sit down with your group members and answer some questions.

1. What main ideas do we want to get across?
2. What activities do we want to do?
3. How should we prepare?
4. Who will do what?

Guidelines for Girl Leaders

Set up some guidelines for yourselves before you meet with the younger girls—otherwise things might get pretty chaotic. Here are some ideas to get you started. Add more of your own.

> " I learned that I was a good teacher. I learned that I could help younger girls. This made me more confident."
>
> —7th-grade girl leader, Tulsa, Oklahoma

- We will listen carefully to the younger girls and try not to drown them out.
- We will model respect for one another.
- We won't interrupt or criticize anyone.
- We will work together as a team.
- We will share leadership positions.
- No meanness or gossiping allowed.

Ground Rules for Younger Girls

Bring a poster to the first session and ask the younger girls to agree to some basic ground rules. Here are some examples:

- Everybody gets time to talk.
- No meanness or teasing allowed.
- We respect different opinions.
- We will try to listen to everyone and not interrupt each other.
- Let's have fun!

Beginnings, Middles, and Ends

Think of each session as having a beginning, a middle, and an end. The beginning can be short: "Hello, here's what we're going to do today," an icebreaker, and so on. So can the end: "It was fun meeting you," "What did you learn?" and so on. The middle's the longest, filled with different activities.

Work in "stations" during the middle and you can do several activities at once. Stations are fun and simple to set up. Let's assume your session is 1 hour long.

1. After hellos and the introduction, older girls divide into three groups. Each group will lead *one* activity at its station.
2. Younger girls divide into three groups, too. Assign them to groups by color code beforehand. Place a (yellow/red/blue) dot on their nametags.
3. Every 15 minutes, the groups of younger girls rotate to a different station. That means each group of older girls teaches their activity three times to three different groups of younger girls.
4. Use the remaining time for your ending.

Skits, Scavenger Hunts, Quizzes

Try to plan a different type of activity at each station. Maybe a panel discussion at station 1, a quiz at station 2, a role play at station 3. Too much of the same thing leads to boredom! Also consider coloring, painting, collage, songwriting, dance, true–false games, storytelling, freewrites, and physical activity to get the younger girls up and moving.

Check out the "Activities" section in this guide. There are more than 20 activities to spark your imagination.

10 Key Ideas

What are 10 things you wish you'd been told about how to live powerfully and healthfully when you were younger? Here are 10 key ideas from the Full of Ourselves program. Some might be complicated for younger girls to understand, so be sure to "translate" into simpler language. What words do little kids use? Can you break "big" ideas into smaller, easier-to-understand pieces?

1. It's who we are on the *inside* that counts most—not what we look like on the outside.
2. Healthy people come in all shapes and sizes!
3. When we become teenagers, our bodies usually change a lot. We typically get taller, heavier, and curvier. This is normal and healthy.
4. Weightism is a mean form of prejudice. It works like racism, except weightism judges people by body size and shape instead of body color.
5. I vow to try my best to understand, respect, and include other people, no matter what they look like. If I see someone being teased for how they look, I will try to be an activist and speak up!
6. Fad diets don't work! If you need to lose weight for health reasons, see a school nurse, doctor, or nutritionist and learn how to have a healthier all-around lifestyle.
7. If you are upset, getting a treat to eat, going on a diet, or shopping won't solve the *real* problem. Figure out what's really "eating" at you.

> ### ❧ Helpful Tip ❧
>
> Use the blank "Session Planning Sheet" (Handout 1) to help you organize! Check out the sample lessons on the following two pages for some good ideas.

8. Fashion models aren't the greatest role models; they don't even really look like their photos! The best role models are women and girls who are *doing* exciting and powerful things.
9. Eat a variety of foods every day. Have you eaten any fruit lately? Veggies? Grains? Protein? Calcium to build strong bones?
10. No matter what your size, it's fun to move and exercise.

Calling All Girl Leaders! Eight Tips for a Winning Class

1. *Pose lots of questions* to get girls talking. Respond to an *answer* with another probing *question*: "How come? Why do you think that? Will you tell me more about that? Does anyone have a different answer?"
2. *Arrive on time.* If you are 7 minutes late, you may walk into a chaotic room—and there goes your good impression, along with a good chunk of the lesson!
3. *Your body language speaks volumes.* Don't move too far away, and try not to turn your back on anyone.
4. *Make eye contact and smile* to help the younger girls to feel welcome and at ease.
5. *Expect the unexpected.* The more fun an activity, the more excitement there will be! And the more the younger girls will want to talk. Or they may want to take the activity in a whole new direction. It's in these moments that group "magic" can occur. So as you map out your session, don't schedule time too tightly. Allow time for spontaneity.
6. *Be on the lookout for anyone who isn't participating* and invite her into the discussion.

"You're not saying much. I'd love to know what you think about ____."

7. *Think of each class as an experiment!* At the end of each class, ask yourself what went well, and why, and what you might do differently next time.

8. *Ask for help whenever you need it.* Give your adult leaders a high sign if anything goes wrong, if you feel stuck, or if you start to feel shaky.

Session # _____ 1 _____ **Date and Time** _____ Thursday, May 8, at 3 o'clock _____

Key Idea(s) We Want to Get Across

Main ideas: It's good to be full of ourselves and throw our weight around in healthy ways. It's who we are on the inside that counts most, not how we look on the outside.

Session Segments	Activity Name/ Approaches (discussion, art, etc.)	Estimated Time/ Timekeeper	Preparation/Supplies	Handouts/ Photocopying	Leaders' Names	Helpers' Names
Beginning	Introductions	5 minutes	Bring snacks!	None	Sylvia and Emma introduce us and explain why we're here.	Everyone else
	Icebreaker	5 minutes	Think of time you felt smart, confident, or brave.			
	Review ground rules.	5 minutes	Newsprint or big paper to write down ground rules; big marker		Francesca leads ground rules.	
Middle: Station 1	Body Statues group movement activity and discussion	15 minutes	None	None	Ayana and Lisa	Everyone else is a "museum goer."
Middle: Station 2	Throw Your Weight Around! Group Pledge	5 minutes	Cut out pledge for each girl.	2 copies of pledge	Cara and Emma review pledge.	Everyone else at Station 2.
	TYWA Drawing (in pairs) art activity	10 minutes	Paper, crayons, fine black markers, glitter glue.	None	Jewel explains drawing.	
Middle: Station 3	Inside/Out brainstorm and discussion	15 minutes	Paper bags, markers, pieces of paper	None	Francesca and Emily	Everyone else at Station 3
End	"What did you learn?" group discussion	5 minutes	None	None	Emma	Everyone else

Session # ___2___ **Date and Time** ___Thursday, May 15, at 3 o'clock___

Key Idea(s) We Want to Get Across

Whatever your body shape and size, it's fun to move and exercise. Take it from us: Your body will change when you become a teenager, and this is normal and healthy. Models are bad role models. Most magazine pictures aren't even real.

Session Segments	Activity Name/ Approaches (discussion, art, etc.)	Estimated Time/ Timekeeper	Preparation/Supplies	Handouts/ Photocopying	Leaders' Names	Helpers' Names
Beginning	Hello icebreaker.	10 minutes	Nametags with color codes	None	Letisha and Cara	Everyone else
Middle: Station 1	Dance Mania: Bring music and teach dance steps to younger girls Fun movement	15 minutes	CD or tape player; favorite dance tapes or CDs	None	Jewel and Kimberly	Everyone else at Station 1
Middle: Station 2	Show and Tell: How Girls' Bodies Change panel disussion and question-and-answer session	15 minutes	Choose moderator and three girls for panel	1 copy of Handout 4: Show and Tell Moderator Script for moderator 3 copies of Handout 5: Show and Tell Panelist Guide for panelists	Moderator: Lisa Panel: Ayana, Cara, and Sophie	Everyone else at Station 2 should sit next to a younger girl and, if needed, help pose questions.
Middle: Station 3	Collage of Faces group art activity	15 minutes	Bring in one or two fashion magazines, scissors, glue	None	Maria and Jane	Everyone else at Station 3 should help tear out faces
End	"What did you learn?" group discussion	5 minutes	None	None	Lisa and Ayana	Everyone else

Throw Your Weight Around! Activities

Plan several activities for one session and teach these at different stations. Feel free to change the activities or make up brand-new ones of your own.

GETTING-TO-KNOW-YOU ACTIVITIES

Confident and Strong

A powerful way for girl leaders and younger girls to introduce themselves.

⭢ One older girl briefly tells about a specific time she felt confident and strong.

⭢ Ask younger girls for a show of hands: "How many of you can think of a time you felt confident and strong?" Ask two or three girls to share.

⭢ Alternate older and younger girls: Each tells of a time she felt confident and strong.

⭢ *Optional:* Write down key words from the conversation on a piece of paper, decorate the border, and hand out copies to the younger girls in your next session.

Favorite Foods

A fun, easy way to learn names.

⭢ Every girl, older and younger, introduces herself by saying her first name and naming a favorite food beginning with the same letter as her name.

The Wind Is Blowing

A great game that gets people moving and lets them find out about common experiences.

⭢ Play this game with the entire group of younger and older girls.

⭢ Ask everybody to stand close together in a circle. One older girl stands in the middle. Everyone except the girl in the middle takes off one of their shoes and places it directly in front of them on the floor. The shoe is a maker for a "spot."

⭢ Explain how the game works:

1. In a loud, clear voice, the girl in the middle says something that is true about herself.
2. Focus on positive things: interests, hobbies, activities, favorite foods, favorite places, people you admire, and so on.
3. The girl in the middle uses the phrase, "The wind is blowing for anybody who . . ." Then she describes one positive thing about herself. (Examples: The wind is blowing for anybody who loves to read. For anybody who likes to swim. For anybody who is an only child. For anybody who plays the violin.)
4. When you hear a statement that is also true for you, you must move to a new spot (behind one of the shoes) in the circle. The girl in the middle finds a new spot, too. If a statement isn't true for you, stay in your spot.
5. Since the circle is one place short, someone will always be left in the middle. This new girl, in a loud and clear voice, now says something positive that is true about herself—"The wind is blowing for anybody who . . ."—and the game continues.

⭢ Make sure everyone is clear about the directions before the game starts. Try one or two practice rounds.

ACTIVITIES ABOUT CONFIDENCE AND POWER

Throw Your Weight Around! Group Pledge

A group pledge to shout out loud.

⮑ *Preparation:* (1) Make one copy of the "Throw Your Weight Around! Pledge" (Handout 2) or write a new pledge of your own! (2) Cut out squares to give to the younger girls.

⮑ Ask the younger girls if they've ever heard the phrase "throw your weight around." What do they think it means?

⮑ Hand out and review copies of the pledge. Does everyone understand what it means? Everyone stands in a big circle and says the pledge loudly together.

> As I grow and change,
> I promise to try to love and respect my body.
> I will stand up for myself and the people I care about.
> I will throw my weight around to make the world a better place!

⮑ *Optional:* Ask the younger girls to decorate the borders with paints, crayons, stickers, and so on.

Stephanie's Ponytail

A terrific story to read to younger girls.

⮑ You can read this story to the younger girls at a station or to the whole group at once.

⮑ *Preparation:* Get a copy of the children's book *Stephanie's Ponytail* by Robert Munsch (New York: Annick Press, 1996). Check your school and local libraries. This is a fun story about a girl who refuses to go along with the crowd—and refuses to let a crowd go along with her!

⮑ Gather the younger girls around in a circle and read this story aloud. Possible discussion questions:

1. What did you notice in this story?
2. Did anything in this story ring true to you?
3. Do girls your age feel a lot of pressure to go along with the crowd?
4. Is there anything wrong with doing "your own thing" and being independent?
5. Is there anything wrong with going along with the crowd?

⮑ Suggest that the younger girls read the story to little sisters or nieces at home.

Inside/Out

A quick way to find out what makes someone special.

⮑ This activity works best when done with the whole group.

⮑ *Preparation:* Bring in plenty of pairs of scissors and a brown paper bag. Decide which older girl will lead the first and last part of the activity.

⮑ Tell the younger girls that you will be doing a fun activity that gets them thinking about the "insides" and the "outsides" of people.

⮑ Begin by asking the large group the following question: "What are words we use to describe how someone looks?" (Examples: tall, short, fat, thin, chubby, brown hair, blonde hair, blue eyes, brown eyes, dark skin, light skin, long hair, straight hair, curly hair, freckles, pimples, birthmark.) Write the girls' answers in bold black marker on the outside of the paper bag.

⮑ Divide everyone into smaller groups. Each girl leader pairs with a younger girl or a couple of younger girls. You are all "sisters"—big sisters and little sisters.

⮑ Each girl leader asks her "little sisters" three questions and lists their answers on a piece of paper. If they have a hard time coming up with an answer, give an example of something that's true for you.

1. Tell me about two things about you that make you special.
2. Tell me about two things you are good at doing.

3. Tell me about two people you really care about and why.

⊃ Cut the girls' answers into separate slips of paper.

⊃ Everyone comes back together in one large group and places the paper slips in the bag.

⊃ Ask one of the younger girls to read the outside of the bag.

⊃ Explain that what's *really* interesting about a person is found on the *inside*. If we only judge someone by how she looks on the outside, we're missing all the really good stuff. Reach into the bag and read some of the "inside" slips. Point out how surprising and interesting all these descriptions are. The insides tell a fascinating story!

Throw Your Weight Around! Poster

A colorful poster about girl power.

⊃ This activity can be done with a small group of girls at a station or with the whole group together.

⊃ *Preparation:* Bring in posterboard and art materials such as colored paper, crayons, glitter, scissors, and anything else you can think of.

⊃ Make a group poster with the younger girls using words and images describing what it means to "throw your weight around."

Powerful Women

A discussion and introduction of women we think are great.

⊃ This activity works well with a small group at a station or with the entire group at once.

⊃ Ask younger girls the following questions to get them thinking before beginning the activity:

1. Can anyone tell me what the word "powerful" means? What else can it mean?
2. Can any of you think of a *person* you know who is "powerful"? What makes him or her powerful?

⊃ Explain that power isn't only about physical strength; you can be powerfully smart or brave or funny, or you can be a powerfully good friend. Give an example of a powerful woman or girl you know in your own life.

⊃ Ask each girl to write down the name of one woman she thinks is *powerful* in some way. This might be a relative, friend, neighbor, a woman from history, or even a fictional character. The woman doesn't have to be famous.

⊃ Ask each younger girl to tell about the woman she admires and why. Point out that these women are "throwing their weight around" in powerful and healthy ways.

⊃ *Optional:* continue to the next activity, "Tree of Strength."

Tree of Strength

An inspiring art project.

⊃ *Preparation:*

1. Photocopy one "Tree of Strength" leaf (Handout 3) for each younger girl.
2. Cut out the leaves and punch a hole in the top of each.
3. Have on hand scissors, hole punches, pens, and paperclips.
4. Bring in a long tree branch with many side branches and twigs. Prop up the tree branch in a coffee can filled with sand or rocks (so that it stands upright like a little tree). The younger girls will hang their leaves from this branch with paperclips.

⊃ Give each girl a leaf handout and explain that you are going to build a "tree of strength." Ask each girl to write the name of her "powerful" woman on the front of the leaf. On the back, ask the girls to write down their own names and one thing they like about themselves.

⊃ Help the girls punch a hole in the top of each leaf and fish a paperclip through the hole.

⊃ Ask the girls, one by one, to come forward and hang their leaf on the tree. Display the tree in a prominent place.

⊃ If you are meeting with the younger girls again, you can assign them the "Powerful Women" homework interview.

A Shot of Self-Confidence

Note-passing that makes everyone feel proud of themselves.

⊃ This activity works best if the younger girls all know one another. It's best done in small groups of five to eight girls.

⊃ Ask everyone to tell you what they know about the word "confidence." Then go around the circle and ask each girl to tell about a time she felt really confident doing something. If anyone hesitates, remind her that this isn't boasting. We all have different strengths, and it's important to recognize them!

⊃ Ask each girl to write her name on the top of a blank sheet of paper. Tell the girls to pass their paper to the person sitting to their right. Explain the directions:

" When you receive a paper with someone else's name on top, take a moment to think about what you really like or admire about that girl—something other than the way she looks or dresses. It might be something about her personality, or her talents, or what she's like as a student or as a friend. Write this down underneath her name. If someone else has written the same thing, try to think of something different."

⊃ After 30 seconds or so, ask the girls to switch papers again, handing their paper to the girl on their right. When papers arrive back to their original owners, tell each girl to write down something she likes or admires about *herself* on the bottom.

⊃ Ask girls to open their papers and read the messages quietly to themselves. Then go around the circle and ask each girl to read one message that she likes from her paper.

⊃ Girl leaders discuss the power of focusing on the positive in ourselves and in others.

Homework: Powerful Women

Girls interview a person they admire.

⊃ Do this homework activity only if you are going to meet with the younger girls again.

⊃ *Preparation:* Write down two interview questions on a piece of paper and make a photocopy for each younger girl:

1. Who is a woman you admire a lot? Why do you admire her?
2. What's something you feel really proud of about yourself?

⊃ Ask each younger girl to name a woman she *knows* whom she admires. Some examples: your mom, grandmother, aunt, teacher, or next-door neighbor.

⊃ Tell the girls to ask this woman if she would sit down for a 15-minute interview. Hand out and read the two interview questions. Do the girls want to add any questions?

⊃ After the interview, the girls can write down or draw the key things they want to remember.

⊃ At the start of the next session, ask each girl to tell whom she interviewed, display her picture, and say one thing that she always wants to remember from the interview.

ACTIVITIES ABOUT SELF-ACCEPTANCE

Show and Tell: How Girls' Bodies Change

An honest panel discussion led by girl leaders.

⊃ This activity works best if done with the entire group of younger girls at once.

⊃ *Preparation:* All girl leaders fill out a copy of "Then and Now: Your Changing Body" (Handout 4) and discuss your answers together as a group.

⊃ Choose one older girl to be the moderator and three older girls to speak briefly about the ways their bodies are changing during the teenage years. Try to choose three girls who have different body shapes and sizes. If possible, include someone whose body hasn't yet changed much at all. Panelists can bring in photos of themselves at the same age as the younger girls and paste or tape them on a collage.

⊃ This activity is a panel presentation. The four older girls sit in a row in front of the "audience" of younger and older girls, who can ask questions at the end.

⊃ The moderator begins by reading "Show and Tell: Moderator Script" (Handout 5).

⊃ After the moderator is done, panel speakers take turns "showing and telling" about their own body changes during puberty. Try to stay positive. Have "Then and Now: Your Changing Body" (Handout 4) in front of you and use "Show and Tell: Panelist Guidelines" (Handout 6) to guide your presentations.

⊃ Does anyone in the audience have any questions? They can ask out loud or write these on slips of paper for the moderator to pose.

⊃ Invite the younger girls to guess who is who on the photo collage.

Hi, Body!

A guided meditation about being your body's best friend.

⊃ This activity can be done with the entire group of younger girls or at a station.

⊃ *Preparation:* (1) Photocopy the "Hi, Body Affirmation" (Handout 7). (2) Cut out one square for each younger girl.

⊃ Introduce the activity to the younger girls like this:

" It's important to remember that your body will be with you for your entire life. So be kind to your body, just like you would be to a good friend. Feed it well, treat it with care, and say nice things to your body so that it—and you!—feel appreciated."

⊃ Ask everyone to lie down on their backs and close their eyes.

" Let's try an experiment. Everyone lie down on your backs, get comfortable, and close your eyes. While I talk, try to 'see' with your imagination what I'm describing. There should be no talking."

⊃ Read the following script *slowly* in a gentle voice, pausing for 5 seconds or so between each sentence to give girls a chance to envision the described scene.

" You are just waking up in the morning . . . Imagine yourself getting up, stretching, brushing your teeth. . . You look in a mirror as you think about what you are going to wear to school . . . Here's what you say to yourself: Hi, body. Hi, me. Good morning! Body, I love you. You are going to carry me through this day. Because of you, I can dance, I can see, I can jump, I can sing. With your help, I can show the world who I am today. I will take really good care of you because you are my only body. And as I love you and respect you, you'll take good care of me. We are allies. You stand up for me and I stand up for you, no matter what anyone else says. We'll be friends through thick and thin. We're friends for life . . . You get dressed, eat breakfast, and head out into your day."

⊃ Ask the girls to open their eyes, stretch, and slowly come back into the circle. What was that like? Could the younger girls "see" themselves? How do they feel now?

⊃ Hand out copies of the "Hi, Body Affirmation" for girls to keep. Invite them to decorate the borders with crayons, stickers, or colored pencils.

ACTIVITIES ABOUT WEIGHTISM AND "BAD BODY TALK"

Weightism: What's That?

A discussion about body prejudice.

⊃ This activity works great with the entire group or at a station.

⊃ Gather the girls in a circle and talk with them about the meaning of the word "weightism." Define the word and give examples from real life. Here's one way to lead into the discussion:

" How many of you know something about Martin Luther King Jr. Day? What is that day about? We all learn how it is unfair and mean to judge or tease other people based on their body color. How many of you have ever heard someone being teased because of their body color? How many of you have ever heard someone being teased because of their body size or shape? What kinds of things do people say?

When you judge a person by the color of his or her skin, it's a form of meanness called 'racism.' And when you judge a person by the shape or size of his or her body, it's a form of meanness called 'weightism.' Weightism is a kind of prejudice. Does anyone know who a bully is? Bullies can pick on others for lots of different reasons. Weightism is when someone gets teased or bullied because of his or her weight—or because of the size and shape of their body."

‿ Why does weightism hurt people's feelings?

‿ Now ask each girl to write down five things she appreciates about her body. Older girls should participate, too. Then go around the circle and each girl reads one reason aloud.

‿ *Optional:* Continue to "Fat Talk," "Inside/ Out," or "'Just Say *No*' to Bad Body Talk: A Group Pledge."

Homework: Fat Talk

An eye-opening "detective" assignment.

‿ Do this activity only if you'll be meeting with the younger girls again. Assign it to the entire group at once.

‿ Ask the girls to be detectives and pay close attention to television shows, movies, and conversations and notice when anyone says something mean or negative about their own or someone else's body. This is called "fat talk" or "bad body talk." What sorts of things do people say? The girls should keep a list.

‿ In the next session, ask the girls if they heard any "bad body talk" and to give examples. Help the girls figure out what they could say or do in response. For example, "That's mean! Don't say that! People come in all shapes and sizes."

ACTIVITIES ABOUT ACTIVISM: PUTTING A STOP TO WEIGHTISM

"Just Say *No*" to Bad Body Talk

A group pledge.

‿ This activity works best if girls have done "Weightism, What's That?" Try this with the entire group at once.

‿ *Preparation:* (1) Photocopy the "Group Pledge to Combat Weightism" (Handout 8). (2) Cut out one square for each younger girl.

‿ Hand out copies of the pledge. Make sure everyone understands what the pledge means, then read it aloud together:

" I promise to try to understand, respect, and include other people, no matter what they look like. People come in all shapes and sizes!"

The Birthday Party

A role play about how to stand up to meanness.

‿ This activity works best with the entire group— the more voices and opinions in the discussion, the better! Five girls are needed for the role play itself.

‿ *Preparation:*

1. Bring in five nametags.
2. Read "The Birthday Party" (Handout 9) and decide whether you'd like to modify or lengthen it.
3. Make five copies of "The Birthday Party."

‿ Ask for five young volunteers to play the characters and narrator. Give each girl a copy of "The Birthday

Party" and make out a nametag for each character. Ask the girls to act out the scene for the "audience."

⮑ At the conclusion, help the younger girls in the audience to identify the roles played by different characters. Here are some questions you might ask:

1. Who's the *bully* in this scene, the mean girl who stirs up a lot of trouble?
2. Are there any *followers*, people who go along with the bully?
3. Why is Jeannie being left out of the party? Do you think this is right?
4. Does anyone speak up or help stop the meanness? This girl is called an *activist*, someone who takes helpful action.

⮑ Ask the younger girls to perform the scene again. Ask audience members to pretend they are at the lunch table, too. What could they say to speak up for Jeannie? If needed, the older girls can demonstrate how to speak up to stop the "body" bullying.

ACTIVITIES ABOUT HEALTHY EATING

The Grocery Cart

A discussion of the difference between "junk" and "power" foods.

⮑ This activity works best at a station. With too many participants, the shopping carts get overloaded.

⮑ *Preparation:* (1) Bring a variety of healthy snacks. (2) On a big piece of paper or newsprint, write out a list of the qualities of "power" foods and "junk" foods:

	"Power" Foods	Junk Foods
What's in it?	Packed with nutrients. Low in fat, salt, and sugar	Packed with additives. Fatty, salty, sugary
What form is it in?	Natural, whole, unprocessed, organic	Processed with chemicals, dyes, preservatives
How is it presented?	Often unpackaged	Often packaged
How is it prepared?	Steamed, broiled, grilled; not much grease	Often fried and greasy

⮑ Lay out snacks for a "snack feast."

⮑ Draw the outlines of four big shopping carts (rectangles, basically, with wheels and handles) on the board or on four pieces of newsprint. Title the carts "Breakfast," "Lunch," "Dinner," and "Snacks."

⮑ Ask the girls, one at a time, to come up and "fill" the carts with the names or drawings of their favorite food items for each meal and snack. They can write down as many items as they want—as long as these would be found in one meal. For example, a girl can write "pepperoni pizza" in the dinner cart, but she can't add "fried chicken" and "hamburgers" since she probably wouldn't eat all of these at one dinner.

⮑ *Rule:* You can't repeat foods that are already in the cart. If your first-choice breakfast food is already in the cart, put a check in front of it, and then add something new.

⮑ Afterwards, display and read down the list of characteristics of "power" foods. Also remind girls how important it is to eat a variety of foods each day; that's how we get all the nutrients we need.

⮑ Ask the girls to count how many of the foods in each shopping cart are "power" foods. Then ask them to check the carts for variety: grains (bread/rice), protein (meat, fish, poultry, eggs, nuts), fruits, and vegetables.

⮑ If any carts are lacking in "power" foods or are short on variety, ask girls what else they could add to the cart to make it more "powerful" and "balanced." Adding these foods to your cart and cupboards is how you create a healthier, more balanced diet.

Eating!

An agree–disagree questionnaire.

⮑ This activity works equally well at stations or with the entire group.

⮑ *Preparation:* (1) Make photocopies of "Eating: A Questionnaire" (Handout 10). (2) Review the "Answer Guide to 'Eating: A Questionnaire'" (Handout 11) before you lead the activity.

⊃ *Note to Leaders:* Don't make any judgments about the younger girls' eating habits.

⊃ Divide the girls into pairs and give each pair one copy of the questionnaire. Pairs take the quiz together. If the girls think a statement is false or don't know the answer, ask them to talk about the reason why with each other.

⊃ When the girls are done, review the questions, asking a pair of girls if they thought the statement was true or false and to explain their reasoning. Provide the right answers using your own knowledge and the "Answer Guide."

⊃ *Optional:* Girls make a group poster about the "most interesting" things they learned from the questionnaire.

Food Pyramid Twister

A new, healthy twist on an old game.

⊃ Play this game at a station with three girls at once. If you have more girls, play more than one game.

Preparation:

1. Draw a picture or cut out magazine photos of three food items from each of the five main food groups: grains, veggies, fruits, milk, and meat/bean. Add one extra item so you have a total of 16 food items.
2. Tape the food items side by side in a 4' × 4' square. If you're in a room with a tiled floor, tape one food in the middle of each tile. You can also tape the items onto the colored circles of an actual plastic "Twister" mat.
3. Create a spinner out of a piece of cardboard divided into five "slices," one for each of the food groups, with each slice subdivided into four: right hand, left hand, right foot, left foot. You can also use the "Twister" spinner and substitute food groups for colors.

⊃ Point out the importance of eating a variety of foods each day; that's how we get all the vitamins and minerals we need.

⊃ Ask three girls to play first. Spin the spinner and call out directions loudly; for example, "Left foot on a veggie," "Right hand on grain." The last girl left standing wins.

ACTIVITIES ABOUT MAGAZINES AND THE MEDIA

Fashion Magazines

A discussion of pros and cons to raise girls' awareness.

⊃ This discussion works best at a station so that all the girls can see the magazine up close.

⊃ Bring a fashion magazine or two and choose a few topics for analysis. Here are some possibilities:

1. *The cover:* Begin by looking at the cover and pointing out the words and images. What are the main messages this magazine is trying to get across? Does it encourage girls to "throw their weight around"—to be smart and brave and strong?
2. *Advertisements:* Point out that most pages in the magazine are ads. Look at *one* ad in particular and its emphasis on *selling* beauty and happiness. Can you go to a store and buy happiness? Or does it come from inside of us?
3. *Photos:* Ask the girls to look through the photos of female models. Which pose looks most ridiculous or uncomfortable? Have everyone try holding this pose for 2 minutes.
4. *Agree or disagree:* Fashion models look the same in person as they do in a magazine. This statement is false. Point out that "seeing is *not* believing" when you read a fashion magazine. Most photographs have been air-brushed to eliminate any "imperfections" (pimples, fat, wrinkles, etc.). Models don't look anything like that when they wake up in the morning!

Get Real!

A collage of faces that gets goofier by the minute.

⊃ *Preparation:* Bring in two or three fashion magazines or use the ones from the last activity. You'll also need lots of pairs of scissors, several gluesticks, a few black pens, and one 8.5" x 11" sheet of paper or posterboard. (Don't use a huge piece because it will take too long to cover with faces.)

⊃ Ask everyone to cut or tear out five faces of a woman or a girl. Then invite girls to glue their faces on the paper to make a collage. The faces should overlap.

⊃ Once the collage is finished, ask girls how "real" these faces appear:

1. Do you think the models look like this when they wake up in the morning?
2. Can you find any pimples? Freckles? Birthmarks? Braces? Glasses? Bad-hair day? Sweat? Bumpy noses? Small eyes? Uneven lips?

⊃ Explain: "These photos are of professional models who have spent hours putting on makeup before being photographed under special lights. Some of them have had plastic surgery to change their looks. And most of the pictures have been air-brushed and touched up with computers."

⊃ Ask girls what they might say or think to remember that these photographs aren't of "real" people. Cut out big letters to spell out one of their suggestions. Glue this "comeback" diagonally across the collage.

⊃ *Note to Leaders:* If the girls have trouble thinking of a "comeback," you might suggest the phrases "Get Real!" or "No Barbies Allowed!" and plaster these letters across the collage.

⊃ Invite girls to draw directly on the faces with black pens to make them look more realistic (add glasses, chipped teeth, zits, etc.).

GET-UP-AND-GO ACTIVITIES

The Human Knot

An activity to get everyone up and moving and working together.

⊃ Try this with the entire group at once, girl leaders included.

⊃ You need an even number of people; one of the girl leaders can bow out if there is an odd number of younger girls in your group.

⊃ Explain the directions:

1. Everyone stand in a circle, shoulder to shoulder, and close your eyes. Reach your right hand into the circle and grab another person's hand—but not your immediate neighbor's.
2. Now reach your left hand into the circle and take hold of a free left hand.
3. Open your eyes and try to untangle. You can talk with one another, change grips, and climb over or under each other's arms, but do not release anyone's hand.

⊃ Sometimes the human knot cannot be completely unwoven. This is okay, as the point of the exercise is to encourage teamwork and communication among the younger girls.

Body Statues

A great way to express yourself without words.

⊃ This activity works best when done with the entire group, but it can also be done at a station if you have five or more girls.

⊃ Clear a space big enough for the younger girls to move around. Divide them into two groups. One group will make a "statue" while the second group acts as "museum-goers."

⊃ One girl leader introduces the activity like this: "In a moment you're going to use your own *bodies* to create a statue in this space. After I announce the title of the statue, take a minute to think about what this title means to you. At that point, any girl can enter the space and strike a pose relating to the title. Then, one girl at a time, others join in and add to the statue with a pose of your own."

⊃ There are three guidelines:

1. Build the statue without speaking a word.
2. When you join the statue, connect in at least one place (touch feet, arms, hands, etc.).
3. Try not to move.

⊃ Assign the title "Be a Good Girl" to the first statue and "Throw Your Weight Around" to the second.

⊃ Once a statue is done, ask the remaining girls (older ones included) to walk around it and comment on what they see. "If this statue could speak, what would it say? How do the people in this statue feel?"

Let's Get Physical

A chance to get everyone up and moving.

⊃ Plan one or more fun, physical activities with the younger girls.

⊃ Jump rope, play kickball, somersault and cartwheel, play Simon Says, and so on. All bodies are designed to move! Whether or not someone's an "athlete," there are tons of ways to move and have fun with our bodies.

⊃ Here are some questions you can ask the younger girls: Do you like to exercise? What are your favorite ways to move around? When do you feel most powerful and alive in your body?

Dance Mania

A dance class and party.

⊃ Bring in your favorite music. Make sure that the lyrics are girl-friendly and appropriate for the younger girls.

⊃ First teach the younger girls some dance steps. Do they know some to teach you?

⊃ Dim the lights and dance!

Throw Your Weight Around!
Session Planning Sheet for Girl Leaders

Session # _____ Date and Time _____

Key Idea(s) We Want to Get Across

Session Segments	Activity Name/ Approaches (discussion, art, etc.)	Estimated Time/ Timekeeper	Preparation/ Supplies	Handouts/ Photocopying	Leaders' Names	Helpers' Names
Beginning						
Middle						
End						

Throw Your Weight Around! Pledge

Photocopy and cut out one square for each girl.

 As I grow and change,
I promise to try to love and respect my body.
I will stand up for myself and people I care about.
I will throw my weight around
to make the world a better place!

 As I grow and change,
I promise to try to love and respect my body.
I will stand up for myself and people I care about.
I will throw my weight around
to make the world a better place!

 As I grow and change,
I promise to try to love and respect my body.
I will stand up for myself and people I care about.
I will throw my weight around
to make the world a better place!

 As I grow and change,
I promise to try to love and respect my body.
I will stand up for myself and people I care about.
I will throw my weight around
to make the world a better place!

 As I grow and change,
I promise to try to love and respect my body.
I will stand up for myself and people I care about.
I will throw my weight around
to make the world a better place!

 As I grow and change,
I promise to try to love and respect my body.
I will stand up for myself and people I care about.
I will throw my weight around
to make the world a better place!

 As I grow and change,
I promise to try to love and respect my body.
I will stand up for myself and people I care about.
I will throw my weight around
to make the world a better place!

 As I grow and change,
I promise to try to love and respect my body.
I will stand up for myself and people I care about.
I will throw my weight around
to make the world a better place!

Tree of Strength

Then and Now: Your Changing Body

★ When you were in 3rd/4th grade, what was your body like? (height, weight, shape, energy level, appetite, moods)

_____

_____

_____

★ How has your body changed between then and now? Be as specific as possible. How hasn't it changed (yet)?

_____

_____

_____

★ Have your interests, activities, and concerns changed? If so, how?

_____

_____

_____

★ What is an embarrassing or awkward "body moment" you've had in the past couple of years?

_____

_____

_____

★ What is something about your body now that you feel good about? (consider energy, strength, stamina, skill, appearance)

_____

_____

_____

Show and Tell: Moderator Script

We're here to talk to you about girls' bodies and how our own bodies have changed since we were your age. I didn't know a lot of this information when I was your age, but I sure wish someone had told me. [*Note:* if someone *did* tell you most of this, let the girls know].

Here are some basic things about becoming a teenager. How much of this is new to you?

★ As you become a teenager, your body changes. You'll probably get bigger and taller and curvier, especially in the hips, thighs, bust, and rear end.

★ You'll put on an extra layer of body fat that boys don't put on. This is normal and healthy for girls and doesn't necessarily mean you get or look fat. There's a reason we put on this extra layer of fat. It's really cool: We are preparing to become women and for the possibility of having babies.

★ Between the ages of 8 and 14, it's normal and healthy for girls to gain 40 pounds. That's an average of 6–7 pounds per year. Unless a doctor says so, going on a diet can be dangerous because your body—your bones, your heart, your hips, your brain—needs to grow!

★ When you first start growing, it might look like you're gaining weight everywhere on your body. Over time, the weight usually redistributes itself mainly to your hips, thighs, and bust.

★ There isn't one set age when your growth spurt will start. It's different for everyone. Some girls begin to develop as young as age 8, while others start as late as age 15. I started at _____. Somewhere between ages 10 and 12 is average.

★ Everyone develops at her own rate. Some girls get taller before they get curvier. Others get curvier and rounder before they get taller. Some girls gain weight before they grow taller. Others grow tall before their weight catches up.

Now you're going to hear what it's been like for our three panelists. The first is girl is . . .

Show and Tell: Panelist Guidelines

Tell the "then" and "now" of your body story. Share what's happened and your feelings. Be honest, but try to stay positive overall! Relax and speak clearly and loudly. Have your "Then and Now" questionnaire in front of you, and use these phrases as jumping-off points:

★ In 3rd/4th grade, I was . . .

★ Now I am . . .

★ These changes happened (period, braces, weight gain, etc.) . . .

★ I am still waiting for . . .

★ One embarrassing or awkward body moment I had was when . . .

★ One thing I really like about my body is . . .

★ I feel great in my body when . . .

Full of Ourselves, *Copyright © 2006 by Teachers College, Columbia University*

"Hi, Body!" Affirmation

Photocopy and cut out one square for each girl.

Hi, Body!

You are going to carry me through this day. Because of you, I can dance, I can see, I can taste, I can sing, I can think. With your help, I can show the world who I am today. I will take really good care of you because you are my only body. And as I love and respect you, you'll take good care of me. We are allies; you stand up for me and I stand up for you, no matter what anyone else says. We'll be friends through thick and thin. We're friends for life.

Hi, Body!

You are going to carry me through this day. Because of you, I can dance, I can see, I can taste, I can sing, I can think. With your help, I can show the world who I am today. I will take really good care of you because you are my only body. And as I love and respect you, you'll take good care of me. We are allies; you stand up for me and I stand up for you, no matter what anyone else says. We'll be friends through thick and thin. We're friends for life.

Hi, Body!

You are going to carry me through this day. Because of you, I can dance, I can see, I can taste, I can sing, I can think. With your help, I can show the world who I am today. I will take really good care of you because you are my only body. And as I love and respect you, you'll take good care of me. We are allies; you stand up for me and I stand up for you, no matter what anyone else says. We'll be friends through thick and thin. We're friends for life.

Hi, Body!

You are going to carry me through this day. Because of you, I can dance, I can see, I can taste, I can sing, I can think. With your help, I can show the world who I am today. I will take really good care of you because you are my only body. And as I love and respect you, you'll take good care of me. We are allies; you stand up for me and I stand up for you, no matter what anyone else says. We'll be friends through thick and thin. We're friends for life.

Hi, Body!

You are going to carry me through this day. Because of you, I can dance, I can see, I can taste, I can sing, I can think. With your help, I can show the world who I am today. I will take really good care of you because you are my only body. And as I love and respect you, you'll take good care of me. We are allies; you stand up for me and I stand up for you, no matter what anyone else says. We'll be friends through thick and thin. We're friends for life.

Hi, Body!

You are going to carry me through this day. Because of you, I can dance, I can see, I can taste, I can sing, I can think. With your help, I can show the world who I am today. I will take really good care of you because you are my only body. And as I love and respect you, you'll take good care of me. We are allies; you stand up for me and I stand up for you, no matter what anyone else says. We'll be friends through thick and thin. We're friends for life.

Group Pledge to Combat Weightism

Photocopy and cut out one square for each girl.

We vow to try our best to
understand, *respect*, and *include* others,
no matter what they look like.
Humans come in *all* shapes, colors, and sizes!

We vow to try our best to
understand, *respect*, and *include* others,
no matter what they look like.
Humans come in *all* shapes, colors, and sizes!

We vow to try our best to
understand, *respect*, and *include* others,
no matter what they look like.
Humans come in *all* shapes, colors, and sizes!

We vow to try our best to
understand, *respect*, and *include* others,
no matter what they look like.
Humans come in *all* shapes, colors, and sizes!

We vow to try our best to
understand, *respect*, and *include* others,
no matter what they look like.
Humans come in *all* shapes, colors, and sizes!

We vow to try our best to
understand, *respect*, and *include* others,
no matter what they look like.
Humans come in *all* shapes, colors, and sizes!

We vow to try our best to
understand, *respect*, and *include* others,
no matter what they look like.
Humans come in *all* shapes, colors, and sizes!

We vow to try our best to
understand, *respect*, and *include* others,
no matter what they look like.
Humans come in *all* shapes, colors, and sizes!

We vow to try our best to
understand, *respect*, and *include* others,
no matter what they look like.
Humans come in *all* shapes, colors, and sizes!

We vow to try our best to
understand, *respect*, and *include* others,
no matter what they look like.
Humans come in *all* shapes, colors, and sizes!

The Birthday Party:
A Scene for Four Characters and a Narrator

NARRATOR: A bunch of 5th-grade girls are sitting at the lunch table, talking excitedly.

JENNIFER: Lilly, I'm *so* excited about your birthday party on Saturday! I can't wait!

YOLANDA: Me, too! Who did you invite?

LILLY: Everybody! Alex, Lilly, Emily, Ayana—

SYLVIA: You didn't invite Jeannie did you?

LILLY: No way! She's a cow. She's really *fat*.

JENNIFER: Yeah, she'd probably eat everything in sight.

YOLANDA: Wait a minute, you guys. We were all playing at Jeannie's house the other day.

LILLY: So what? This is *my* birthday party, and I don't want anybody fat or ugly to spoil it. I want it to be perfect.

NARRATOR: No one speaks up for Jeannie. What would *you* do?

Eating: A Questionnaire

Are the following statements (**T**)rue or (**F**)alse? Circle the letter you think is correct.

T   F   1. Eating makes you smart.

T   F   2. All fat people overeat. That's why they're fat.

T   F   3. Eating makes you strong.

T   F   4. Everyone should eat the same size portions at lunch.

T   F   5. Fat in foods is bad for you.

T   F   6. Diets in magazines are bad for your health.

T   F   7. It's normal for teenage girls to gain weight and add an extra layer of body fat.

T   F   8. When you're upset, getting a treat to eat is a good way to feel better.

T   F   9. Exercise is the main thing that influences how tall or short, fat or thin, you become.

T   F   10. Exercise is only for athletes.

Answer Guide to "Eating: A Questionnaire"

1. **TRUE. Eating makes you smart.** Food provides fuel for the brain. It's like the gas you put in a car to make the engine run. If you don't eat a meal, you get tired more easily and it's harder to think. Without essential nutrients, your brain has to work much harder to pay attention both in and outside of school. So if you skip lunch, it will be harder to learn.

2. **FALSE. People can get fat for many different reasons.** Some people do eat too much junk food or eat for emotional reasons when their bodies aren't really hungry. But the size and shape of someone's body is determined by a lot of other factors, too: their family background, the speed of their metabolism, their age, and their eating and exercise habits. Some people get fat because they've gone on and off so many diets, their bodies have gotten confused. But whether someone's fat or thin, teasing them about their body shape is mean and unfair. If someone needs to lose weight for health reasons, the best thing to do is talk with a doctor, nurse, or nutritionist and make a plan to change not only her eating habits but also her entire lifestyle.

3. **TRUE. Eating makes you strong.** Eating helps you run faster, jump higher, swim farther, and think better. Eating makes you more graceful and better coordinated. Eating also gives you the energy you need to get through the day. Your bones are still growing, so it's really important that you eat enough calcium (milk, cheese) and protein (nuts, fish, chicken, meat) to help develop strong bones.

4. **FALSE. Everyone needs to eat different-sized portions of food because everyone's body has different needs.** Only *you* know how hungry you are, how active you are, how high or low your energy is, and what you've already eaten that day. If you are a gymnast, a ball player or someone who loves to run around, you need more food than someone who sits. The best way to figure out what size portion of food is right for you is to tune in to your own appetite—*not* look at your friend's plate.

5. **FALSE. Healthy fat is an important part of a healthy diet.** We all need to eat some fat to stay healthy. Fat helps build a strong heart and strong bones. Fat helps keep you from getting irritable. It also makes your hair shiny and your skin soft.

6. **TRUE. Most diets in magazines are bad for your health.** They can't be trusted because they aren't supervised by a doctor or a nutritionist. If someone is overweight and needs to diet for health reasons, she needs to see a doctor, school nurse, or nutritionist who can help her make healthy changes to her diet and overall lifestyle.

7. **TRUE. Teenage weight gain is normal and necessary for good health.** All girls have a growth spurt. Sometimes it starts as early as third grade; other girls don't start until age 14. But all of us need to grow and gain weight to become women. Teenage girls also put on an extra layer of body fat that boys don't put on. This is because our bodies are preparing for the possibility of having children.

8. **FALSE. When you're upset, eating will not take away the real source of the upset.** Do any of you ever eat when you're upset? Most people do at times. But eating when you're bored, mad, lonely, or frustrated doesn't help you deal with the *real* problem and can lead to weight gain. For instance, if you're upset with someone, the best thing to do is tell him or her. A double-scoop sundae might taste good, but it won't solve the problem with your friend.

9. **FALSE. We all inherit our basic physical traits from our parents and grandparents.** For instance, you might inherit your eye color from your mom, your curly hair from your dad, your adult height from your dad, and your body shape from your mom or one of your grandparents. How much you eat and exercise has *some* influence, but not as much as you might think.

10. **FALSE. Exercise is for everyone!** Our bodies are made to move: walk, dance, run, skip, ski, flip, shoot baskets, swim, surf, bike, play ball, you name it. Whatever your shape or size, it's fun to move and exercise.

About the Authors

Catherine Steiner-Adair, Ed.D, is a clinical psychologist, school consultant, author, and teacher who has worked in the fields of education and psychology for 25 years. Catherine's clinical work and research in the areas of girls' development and understanding, treating, and preventing eating disorders is internationally recognized. She has consulted to over 250 independent and public schools as well as camps, nonprofit organizations, and clinical/academic institutions. In addition to eating disorders prevention and treatment, her areas of expertise include risk and resilience factors in children's development, the impact of culture on gender identity, boys' and girls' social relationships, and a range of topics concerning education and parenting. She was on the teaching faculty of the Family Institute of Cambridge and served as a school psychologist and teacher at Phillips Academy Andover and the Dana Hall School.

Catherine has been a featured expert in various documentaries, including *Still Killing Us Softly* and the Discovery Channel's *National Body Challenge,* and in many popular magazines, including *Vogue, Seventeen,* and *Child.*

Catherine is currently a clinical instructor in Psychology at McLean Hospital and in the Department of Psychiatry at the Harvard Medical School. She also is in private practice where she works with adolescents, adults, couples, and families.

Lisa Sjostrom, Ed.M., is an accomplished writer, teacher, trainer, and nationally recognized program designer who has devoted her professional life to helping kids thrive. Lisa has worked with and on behalf of children for nearly two decades, first as a teacher in K–12 classrooms and then as a curriculum designer at leading institutions including Harvard University, Wellesley College, and the Ms. Foundation for Women. Along with eating disorders prevention, her areas of expertise include bullying prevention, character education, community building, and gender equity.

Lisa's widely-acclaimed curricula are making a positive difference in schools and communities across the country. She is author/co-author of the following: *Bullyproof: A Teacher's Guide on Teasing and Bullying in School, Citizenship in Action: Bringing Civics to Life in Middle School, Flirting or Hurting: A Teacher's Guide to Student-to-Student Sexual Harassment in School, Making Connections: Building Gender Dialogue and Community in Middle School, The Principals' Guide to Open Circle,* and *Working It Out: A Teacher's Guide to Take Our Daughters to Work Day.*

Lisa is currently a research associate in Psychology at McLean Hospital and in the Department of Psychiatry at the Harvard Medical School. She is also the director of Helping Kids Thrive, an educational consulting firm.